THE LEAVEN OF LOVE

The Leaven of Love

A Development of the Psychoanalytic Theory and Technique of Sándor Ferenczi

BY IZETTE DE FOREST

ARCHON BOOKS
HAMDEN, CONNECTICUT
1965

Reprinted, 1965, by permission
in an unaltered and unabridged edition

Library of Congress Catalog Card Number: 65-14585
Printed in The United States of America

In Memory of My Husband
Alfred Victor de Forest
Devoted Friend of Sándor Ferenczi

CONTENTS

FOREWORD

Yielding to the insistence of her pupils and professional friends, Izette de Forest brings here together in one volume her publications of the last decade. The book as a whole is unique in the psychoanalytic literature. It is the reflection of a life work; of a personal devotion and dedication to the goal of relieving human suffering, of the freeing of neurotically entangled human lives. It is the vital expression of a loving and compassionate heart made effective in practice by a trained technical skill and by the blessings of native intuitiveness and wisdom.

The original aim of the author was not to create a closely knit system of analytic theory and practice; nor are the papers which form the basis of this volume the results of cut-and-dried research projects. Her purpose has been to find more effective ways of helping her patients, through an ever-deepening understanding of the human being in his neurotic struggle. The chapters of this book comprise original and penetrating formulations of the understanding reached by her and of refinements of technique as they shaped themselves in her day-to-day therapeutic work.

In spite of the absence of a premeditated intention to create a well-rounded system, the work as a whole shows remarkable unity and a spontaneous systematic evolution of ideas. The unity of the work lies in its basic orientation: a conviction of the infinite value of every human individual; a clear perception of the healthy fundamental urge for self-preservation and for the protection of personal integrity, both of which lie at the root of the neurotic defensive structures. The clear perception of the native health, strength, and value of the person—of which the therapist should never lose sight, whatever the degree and severity of the neurotic manifestations may be—offers the basis for the hope of reconstruction and "final reconciliation."

This basic orientation is credited by the author to Sándor Ferenczi. Little is known of the final therapeutic outlook of Ferenczi as it was taking shape in the last years of his life. I believe, however, that Mrs. de Forest with her keen intuition, and because of the emotional kinship with her teacher and friend, correctly sensed the path that Ferenczi was taking. She has followed this path in her therapeutic work and in her writings and has enriched it with her own wisdom and understanding.

No one who is acquainted with the complexities and vicissitudes of psychoanalytic therapy will fail to acknowledge this book as the document of a devoted and courageous endeavor, and to receive from it stimulation and valuable instruction.

ANDRAS ANGYAL

PREFACE

THROUGHOUT some twenty-five years of experience in the practice of psychoanalysis, I have endeavored to apply and to develop the theories and techniques of Sándor Ferenczi. It is my hope that this book, which summarizes this endeavor, will afford a wider understanding of certain elements in psychotherapy of which the importance has not yet, in my opinion, been sufficiently recognized. Since the insights at the heart of Ferenczi's psychoanalytic method have significant implications for the whole range of mental health and human relations, it is also my hope that the book will be of value and interest to the general reader, as well as to persons especially concerned with problems of guidance and counseling—ministers, doctors, teachers, social workers. Though parts of the work were addressed in the first instance to the members of my own profession, I have used the technical vocabulary as sparingly as possible, and have provided at the back of the book a glossary of definitions for readers unfamiliar with essential terms in the field.

It was my privilege to be in analysis with Sándor Ferenczi in 1925–1927 and 1929, at the time when he was becoming acutely aware of his dissatisfaction with some of the crucial aspects of the Freudian approach, and was endeavoring to discover a more basic understanding of neurotic needs and of the art of uncovering and restoring the underlying inborn personality. My therapeutic analysis and training under his guidance were followed throughout his last years by conversations and discussions on the subject of psychoanalysis. The value of what I learned from him I thought I then appreciated, but in my subsequent professional work I have discovered more deeply the true significance of his theories, and have devoted my psychoanalytic practice to their development. In this I was constantly enriched by my husband's interest and encouragement.

These theories and their exemplification in practice I have described in the central portions of this book, adding to them my own findings. In introducing them, I have given a short account of Ferenczi's life and of his lifelong friendship with Sigmund Freud. The last three difficult years of this friendship are a remarkable illustration of Ferenczi's depth of nature—a special fusion of self-reliance, humility, and love, which impelled his search in psychotherapeutic theory and technique. In the last section of the book I have dealt with a form of consciousness which I consider religious, and have outlined what I believe to be the similarity between the love given to the patient in psychotherapy and divine love, the evolving interpretation of which is traced throughout Biblical history.

This book includes a number of papers previously published in various journals. These papers have been somewhat revised, some passages have been omitted and new material added. My work here has been assisted by my friends, Georgina Johnston and John Rackliffe, and I am very thankful to them for this lightening of my task. Four chapters are wholly new.

Ferenczi's stepdaughter, Mrs. Elma P. Laurvik, and two of his former colleagues, Dr. Sandor Lorand and Dr. Sandor Rado, have furnished me with details concerning Ferenczi's life. I am grateful for their interest and their help.

F. Alexander Magoun, my husband's close friend and mine, has given me patient and constructive criticism in the composition of this book. The unavoidably technical theories have greatly benefited from the simplicity and warmth of his approach. These theories are generally applicable to human life, and I am thankful for Professor Magoun's expert cooperation in reading the manuscript and more clearly defining this applicability.

To the Friends' New Testament Discussion Group, of Cambridge, Massachusetts, led with kindly skill by William Matchett, I owe instruction and inspiration. Here the members listened in eagerness to each other's interpretations, in the belief that "There is that of God in every man."

With Andras Angyal I have discussed at length the relation between Sándor Ferenczi's theory of the therapeutic gift of love, Erich Fromm's theory of the development of the patient's integrity of personality, and the basic tenets of religious faith. To Dr. Angyal I owe deep and affectionate gratitude.

Throughout a decade of association with Erich Fromm, as both pupil and friend, I have been greatly helped in affirming my belief in man's integrity and in relating this belief to Ferenczi's wish to cherish the neurotic patient back to health. Dr. Fromm has stressed, both in his professional work and in his writings, the importance of the development of individuality. He has called urgent attention to the effect of social pressure in initiating neurotic organization. He has emphasized the need for an ethical point of view in psychoanalytic technique and theory, since man is in himself moral with his essential value standards. These standards are submerged in neurosis and must be rescued for health in order to assist the neurotic patient to achieve his innate personality structure.

Dr. Fromm's clear understanding of the ethic in neurosis and his belief in human goodness have reinforced my own therapeutic findings and also my religious faith. I am deeply indebted to him for his loving and inspiring stimulation and support.

Sky Farm
Marlborough
New Hampshire
September 13, 1953

IZETTE DE FOREST

ACKNOWLEDGMENTS

GRATEFUL acknowledgment of the kind permission to include selections from papers already published, for chapters in this book, is made to the following journals:

Character and Personality
The International Journal of Psycho-Analysis
Inward Light
The Journal of Pastoral Care
The Journal of Clinical Psychopathology
Pastoral Psychology
The Psychiatric Quarterly
The Psychiatric Quarterly Supplement
Psychiatry
The Psychoanalytic Review

THE LEAVEN OF LOVE

Introduction

SÁNDOR FERENCZI

His Life

Sándor Ferenczi was born at Miskolcz, Hungary, July 7, 1873. He died in Budapest, in his charming home in the Buda hills, on May 22, 1933, of pernicious anemia.

His parents were well-to-do, owning the largest bookstore in the city of Miskolcz. They were cultivated and liberal in their interests, unusually enlightened in the freedom and companionship which they gave to their eleven children. The family life was gay and spontaneous, with a love of humorous adventure, and devoted to the enjoyment of scholarship, of music, drama, poetry, and of languages, both ancient and modern. Ferenczi, with his six brothers, graduated from the local *Gymnasium*. Even in his high school days his interest and imagination were attracted to the new academic field of psychology. He often spoke later with amusement of the experiments in hypnotism which he performed upon the clerks in the family bookstore. This interest in psychology may have been instrumental in leading him to enroll as a medical student in Vienna.

Receiving his medical degree in 1894, he started his practice as physician in the Austro-Hungarian Army. After his year of compulsory military service he interned in the various hospitals in Budapest, notably St. Rokus Hospital. There he specialized in neurology and neuropathology, also developing his skill in hypnotism and autosuggestion. In 1900, as a neurologist, he opened an office in Budapest.

An omnivorous reader, he had, in the early days of his neurological practice, discovered Freud's *The Interpretation of Dreams* (*Die Traumdeutung*). This book was the turning point in his career; for its original and exciting ideas so impressed him that he immediately began using the psychoanalytic method in the treatment of his patients. On the title page of his copy of *Die Traumdeutung* he wrote the words *"Aere Perennius"*—"more lasting than bronze." The next step along the new path was a letter in 1907 to Professor Freud, asking the privilege of calling upon him in Vienna in order to pay his respects. Freud then invited him to join the psychoanalytic group in Vienna, at that time a small private society. These two brilliant minds were at once drawn to each other and an intimate friendship was established that continued throughout their lives. Both men discussed with absolute frankness their scientific and personal problems and their mutual interests. These were not only professional interests but included their pleasure in all natural phenomena—as, for example, their delight in the study of mushrooms. They spent many vacations together and in 1909 Freud asked Ferenczi to accompany him on his trip to the United States, where he had been invited to give a course of lectures at Clark University. Freud sent many patients to Ferenczi at the beginning of his analytic practice, and soon Ferenczi had a well-established clientele of his own, patients frequently coming to him from America.

In the First World War he served in Pécs, a small garrison city in Hungary, as Captain in the Medical Corps—impatient that for the time being he could not continue practicing the new psychoanalytic therapy.

In 1919 Ferenczi married. This was a marriage blessed with happiness throughout the rest of his life. His wife had formerly lived for a few years in Miskolcz and they had met again in Budapest. There were no children of the marriage, but Mrs. Ferenczi's two daughters by a former marriage were an ever-present joy to Ferenczi. This was furthered by the marriage of his brother, a banker in Budapest, to the younger daughter.

The organization of yearly meetings of psychoanalysts, gathered together from several European countries, was in part due to Ferenczi's initiative. At the First Psycho-Analytical Congress, held in Salzburg in 1908, he read his first technical paper, "Psycho-Analysis and Education." It was at the Second Psycho-Analytical Congress, held in Nuremberg in 1909, that he made the motion to organize the International Psycho-Analytical Association. He attended the Congresses faithfully, often giving papers, and was elected President of the Association in 1918 at the Fifth Psycho-Analytical Congress in Budapest. In 1929, at the Oxford Congress, he was nominated again to the presidency but deferred to Max Eitingon. In 1913 he and three colleagues formed the Hungarian Psycho-Analytical Society. Although the Society was relatively inactive during the war, it grew rapidly in the postwar years, gaining an importance in the psychoanalytic world out of all proportion to the size of the country, and a wide reputation for its therapeutic work and research. As long as he lived Ferenczi was its permanent president. A Psycho-Analytical Clinic was established in Budapest in 1930.

In 1926–1927 Ferenczi was invited by the New School of Social Research in New York to give a course of lectures on psychoanalysis. This invitation he accepted with pleasurable anticipation, bringing Mrs. Ferenczi with him for the eight months' visit. During these months in the United States he continued treatment of his American patients, began treatment with new patients, held seminars on the practice of psychoanalysis, and worked with several American psychiatrists as students in training. Dr. and Mrs. Ferenczi spent most of their week ends with us in our home in Connecticut, to the great joy of all my family. Ferenczi had an unusual understanding of children and shared their delight in mischievous fun as well as in more constructive projects. I remember vividly the family gatherings when we listened to Ferenczi and my husband spinning their dazzling webs of spontaneous phantastic thought, vying with each other in originality and humor.

Throughout his life Ferenczi was a loyal adherent, a devoted friend, and an ardent co-worker of Sigmund Freud. His most treasured memories were of the walking trips in Italy and in the Semmering in the early days of psychoanalysis, when together they tested the Professor's latest theories, offering themselves to each other as subjects and mutually stimulating further incursions into the realm of human personality. To this foundation of loyal devotion and deep affection for his master and friend, Ferenczi brought his own personal gifts.

Of these, his sensitivity to human suffering and his high degree of imaginative power were outstanding. Wherever his intuition and insight led him in his wish to relieve the burden of neurosis, there he must follow. No stone must be left unturned, no path unexplored. To him failure was but a signal that somewhere, somehow, the successful way could be found. Patience, endurance, and a constant determination to learn and to increase his skill, all these furthered his explorations. How most deeply to touch the kernel of emotional conflict and most thoroughly to eradicate it became the central problem of his life. "In no time his fame as an analyst for hopeless cases became world-wide and soon he was regarded all the world over as 'the haven of lost cases.' His many technical experiments were the reaction to this demand for help."[1]

In the long years of his close association with Professor Freud, Ferenczi wrote many papers dealing with his research in psychoanalysis. These discussed his theories of personality and of neurotic symptoms and behavior and described his therapeutic findings. Many of these papers, the products of his early and middle years of practice, have been collected in book form.[2] During the last few years of his life he wrote nothing except notes on his observations, hurriedly scribbled on scraps of paper, and one completed paper, "Confusion of Tongues Between the Adult and the Child," read at the Twelfth International Psycho-Analytical Congress in Wiesbaden, September, 1932.

Ferenczi was a therapist of the first rank, dedicated to his search for an increasingly efficacious psychoanalytic process. His

[1] Michael Balint, "Sándor Ferenczi, obiit 1933," *International Journal of Psycho-Analysis,* "Ferenczi Number," Vol. XXX, Part 4, 1949.

[2] A bibliography of the writings of Sándor Ferenczi, including posthumous papers, can be found in *Further Contributions to the Theory and Technique of Psycho-analysis* by Sándor Ferenczi, compiled by John Rickman, pp. 451–469 (Basic Books, Inc., New York, 1952, 1953). The following books and volumes of collected papers by Ferenczi are now available in English translation:

Sex in Psycho-analysis; originally entitled *Contributions to Psychoanalysis,* by S. Ferenczi (Richard G. Badger, Boston, 1916; Basic Books Publishing Company, New York, 1950).

The Development of Psycho-analysis by S. Ferenczi and Otto Rank; *Nervous and Mental Disease Monograph Series,* No. 40 (Nervous and Mental Disease Publishing Company, New York, 1925).

Psychoanalysis and the Psychic Disorder of General Paresis by Stefan Hollós and S. Ferenczi; *Nervous and Mental Disease Monograph Series,* No. 42 (Nervous and Mental Disease Publishing Company, New York, 1925).

Further Contributions to the Theory and Technique of Psycho-analysis by Sándor Ferenczi; The International Psycho-Analytical Library, No. 11 (Hogarth Press and the Institute of Psycho-Analysis, London, 1926, 1950, 1951; Basic Books, Inc., New York, 1952, 1953).

Thalassa: A Theory of Genitality by Sándor Ferenczi (Psychoanalytic Quarterly, Inc., New York, 1938).

endless attempts at improvement led to revolutionary changes. But he published none of his final theories and findings. He devoted himself instead to devising and clinically testing radical departures from his earlier technical procedures, often describing his ideas and the results of his work in discussions with friends and colleagues.

His last therapeutic theory, the contribution of his full maturity, can be summarized in a sentence or two. Like many of the "late" works of genius in all fields, it shows a radical and absolute simplicity: *The indispensable healing power in the therapeutic gift is love.* When this love is offered with openness and honesty, in the service of expert skill, it works as leaven: a leaven which lightens and effectively dissipates the burden of neurotic suffering and brings renewal of integrity and health.

Ferenczi and Freud

The long and close friendship of Ferenczi and Freud is a fact and a tradition of which the psychoanalytic school can be proud. That the threatened "fatal break" did not occur is a second fact for which it can be thankful. Both the long friendship and the avoidance of its destruction stand out as exceptional occurrences in the early years of psychoanalysis in Vienna.

Three other brilliant pupils, colleagues, and friends of Sigmund Freud—Jung, Adler, and Rank—felt it necessary to leave the circle of disciples that gathered around the Professor; Jung and Adler in the early days of this association, and Otto Rank, a beloved young pupil, at a later period. These were men of great originality. It proved impossible for them to develop ideas that differed radically from those of Professor Freud and, at the same time, to remain members of the group—and this in spite of the fact that they retained basic points in Freud's original theories.

Interpretations which suggest that Freud could brook no rivalry or that these three outstanding pupils could not endure his severe criticism seem too oversimplified to reflect the full reality. It is more probable that both factors helped to cause the severance of the relationships.

"The early history of psycho-analysis is full of tragic events and tragic lives. Indeed it was the heroic age of our movement. Perhaps the most tragic, the most moving history of all is that of Sándor Ferenczi.

"This is a bold statement. Neither the many friends, won by his radiant lovable personality, nor the inexhaustible wealth of his ideas, nor the unchallengeable successes of his scientific career, seem enough to justify such an opinion. Although he was Freud's junior by twenty-one years, Ferenczi became in an incredibly short time, a matter of only a few months, perhaps the closest friend of the master, and was for many years his inseparable companion on his jealously guarded holiday journeys. Among the quickly growing hosts of analysts Ferenczi attained —as a matter of course—a special place of respect and he was loved and admired all the world over by everyone. Except for Freud, perhaps no one contributed so many and such fundamentally new ideas to our science; Ferenczi's contributions belong, today more than ever, to the classical works of Psycho-Analysis."[3]

Ferenczi, as brilliant a therapist, research worker, and theorist as Adler, Jung, and Rank—possibly even more brilliant—found it not only inconceivable but a denial of the fervent desire of his heart to give up his loyal adherence to Professor Freud. In

[3] Michael Balint, "Sándor Ferenczi, obiit 1933," *International Journal of Psycho-Analysis,* "Ferenczi Number," Vol. XXX, Part 4, 1949.

spite of Freud's increasingly harsh criticism and disapproval of his research and findings, Ferenczi maintained his position as admiring pupil and colleague. This auspicious fact was not due to any lack of radically conflicting views; for Ferenczi throughout his professional life changed his therapeutic approach from year to year, not only differing from that of Freud but from that of his own earlier procedures. These changes he steadfastly supported with careful observation and substantial theories.

From a "passive" therapist he became determinedly "active." In the Freudian analytic technique the patient was a solitary donor of the history of his sufferings and the therapist a mirror, reflecting, but not participating in, this cathartic process. This passive attitude of the analyst allowed no room for the therapeutic relationship of natural tenderness and frankness which Ferenczi increasingly deemed essential. It created instead an atmosphere of distance and mystery. It provided for the analyst a superior and powerful position, often similar to that of the patient's parents from whom he might have suffered disastrously. To help induce a relationship wholly unlike that of the earlier harmful experiences, Ferenczi allowed no artificial distance to intervene between him and his patients, for he thought of them as friends. Instead he gave generously whatever he considered was needed in words and behavior. With humility he invited from his patients any and all expressions of distrust, dislike, and even abusive criticism. He confessed his shortcomings and his regret for them, acknowledging his mistakes. He freely voiced his affectionate regard and beneficent hopes. Psychoanalytic treatment, he thought, should take place as a natural, concerned, personal relationship, a part of life, not something removed from the experience of everyday living. This friendly reassuring environment must under every circumstance be honest. And it must fulfill the essential purpose of eventually reaching back into the traumatic and pre-traumatic experience in the patient's life.

A note dated November 11, 1932, reads:

"Analyses which are carried through on the level of reality never reach the depth of the processes of splitting. Yet each succeeding development depends on the way it occurs (on its vehemence), on the time factor, and on the conditions, of the original splitting (primal repression). Only in earliest childhood, or before the original splitting, was anyone 'one with himself.' Deep analysis must go back under the level of reality into pre-traumatic times and traumatic moments, but one cannot expect a proper resolution unless this time the resolution is different from the original one. Here intervention is necessary (regression and new beginning). Cf. the kindly understanding, the 'permission to give vent' and the encouraging calming reassurance."

This short but significant note gives hint of Ferenczi's constant concern with a deeper understanding of personality and of the therapeutic technique by which this understanding can be reached. The needs of the psychoneurotic sufferer were in his mind reduced to an equation far simpler than in the Freudian method of that time. But their satisfaction was far more difficult to effect. That the patient needed love, and only love, was his belief. But how to give this needed love, and in what form, was the complex question.

Part of the answer, he believed, lay in the personality and character development of the therapist. His change of emphasis in regard to the relationship of analyst and patient did not result in a rejection of Freud's theory of the significance of the patient's "transference." In fact the transference became in Ferenczi's hands even more vital and basic, for he saw in it the central therapeutic implement. He found that it could be used to bring about the necessary reliving and resolving of the original trauma which had initiated the neurosis, with reconciliation as the final outcome. A further change from the Freudian technique consisted in assisting the patient to create, with the analyst, a new and successful form of relationship, which contained none of the elements of the neurotic transference but which allowed the constitutional nature of the patient to be found and to develop.

These ingenious and radical conceptions took form in Ferenczi's latest years and were but a few of his many departures from the theory and practice of Freud. In each instance his theoretical exploration was grounded in reality. As he wrote to Freud, October 10, 1931: "I am above all empiric in my approach (you may think this strange in view of the mass of daring theoretical propositions I have launched). My ideas always originate in the variations of response to treatment shown by my cases and I confirm or reject my hypotheses by reference to this material. I am also very careful as regards publication; perhaps too much so—so that in the intervals it may appear to many as if I had vanished from the scene."[4] But each innovation, together with the rationale underlying it, Ferenczi communicated to his friend, frequently making visits to Vienna from his home in Budapest for this purpose.

That many of Ferenczi's ideas displeased Freud is well known. In one letter Ferenczi refers to Freud's assertion, among other charges, that his "latest views . . . seem incapable of leading to any 'desirable goal.' " And in a letter from Budapest in January, 1932, Ferenczi writes:

LIEBER HERR PROFESSOR:

The tone of gentle reproach in your letter is, I am sure, deserved. To be quite frank, I was prepared for much worse. . . . Of late years it is true that I have been very much, perhaps far too much, ab-

[4] These letters from Ferenczi to Freud, dating from 1931, 1932, and 1933, were translated by Joan Rivière and published in the "Ferenczi Number" of the *International Journal of Psycho-Analysis*, Vol. XXX, Part 4, 1949.

sorbed and preoccupied in my work, trying to understand my patients. But whatever the motives which lead to this kind of isolation, it is not necessarily a bad or worthless thing in itself; probably everyone has to go through such periods, though it is true that in my case they have developed rather late—as you once said, rather like a deferred puberty. . . .

Mit vielen herzlichen Grüssen auch an alle Ihre Lieben,

Ihr ergebener,
FERENCZI

His final letter, written in March, 1933, from his deathbed in Budapest, reads as follows:

LIEBER HERR PROFESSOR:

Only a few short lines to tell you that the date of your birthday is continually in our mind. Let us hope that this next year will not bring forth such unpleasant events as the last has done.

I am much the same; my symptoms remain as they were. I do my best to put some faith in the optimistic views expressed by my doctors.

Ihr,
S. and G. FERENCZI

With this letter was one from Mrs. Ferenczi:

LIEBER HERR PROFESSOR:

The few lines here written in bed by Sándor will show you that he is still far from being himself. I don't know what to believe or what to hope. Lévy hopes for a rapid improvement—and I want to *believe him*. My heart is full of sadness.

I wish you every happiness on your birthday, lieber Herr Professor.

Herzliche Grüsse sendet Ihrer Familie,

Ihre getreue,
FRAU G.

It may be asked, What in Sigmund Freud's personality prevented the final blow which threatened to bring this long-enduring friendship to an end many times during the last three years of Ferenczi's life? It is perhaps more pertinent for us to ask, What in Sándor Ferenczi's personality was able to withstand this friend's severe criticism—and indeed almost his enmity—of these last years? Why did he not, like Adler, Jung, and Rank, break away to institute a new school of psychoanalysis?

In spite of their many fundamental differences of opinion, Ferenczi revered Freud's brilliant genius. His capacity for love and loyalty was unusually genuine and profound. Regardless of any disapproval or hostility which he might arouse in his colleagues, he believed intensely in his own integrity. And he had thorough confidence in his desire and efforts to find the core of neurotic suffering and to relieve it. He also had an unusual degree of resilience and endurance in meeting and using adverse criticism. Hence he felt no compulsion to make an aggressive defense of his contributions. If this interpretation of Ferenczi's personal gifts is correct, he must simply have loved Freud too deeply to break with him. No criticism from anyone—patient, colleague, or even his beloved master—much as it injured his heart, could either change his attitude toward his work or his devoted loyalty toward his patients, his friends, and Freud.

In his last paper, Ferenczi stressed the constructive role of adverse criticism, urging that analysts take seriously the hostility and verbal attacks of their patients, not brushing such expressions aside as "resistance." "I started to listen to my patients when, in their attacks, they called me insensitive, cold, even hard and cruel, when they shouted at me: 'Help! Quick! Don't let me perish helplessly!' Then I began to test my conscience in order to discover whether, despite all my conscious good intentions, there might after all be some truth in these accusations." He spoke of the need of the therapist to be "above all . . . really well analysed, right down to 'rock bottom.' We must have learnt to recognize all our unpleasant external and internal character traits in order that we may be really prepared to face all those forms of hidden hatred and contempt that can be so cunningly disguised in our patients' associations." He spoke of the benefit of admitting therapeutic errors and by such admission earning the confidence of the patient. He compared whatever attitude the analyst might discover in himself of hypocrisy or dislike for the patient to those attitudes in the patient's parents which led originally to the neurotic illness; and he urged that these be confessed to the patient, thus assisting in the creation of a new and sincere relationship. As he stated: "The setting free of his [the patient's] critical feelings, the willingness on our part to admit our mistakes and the honest endeavor to avoid them in the future, all these go to create in the patient a confidence in the analyst. *It is this confidence that establishes the contrast between the present and the unbearable traumatogenic past,* the contrast which is absolutely necessary for the patient in order to enable him to re-experience the past no longer as hallucinatory reproduction but as an objective memory." (Italics in the original.)

An understanding of the constant unfolding of Ferenczi's character and of his humble self-dedication to his patients makes it possible for us to comprehend his refusal to be defeated in his friendship with Freud. In his therapeutic practice he invited criticism from his patients and used whatever truth he could find in it to benefit his own development and theirs. In like manner he listened to Freud's criticism, though its bitterness wounded him deeply, examined it, and accepted and acknowledged whatever seemed to him applicable; hoping against hope that, as with his patients, his beloved friend would in time finally reestablish his trust in him. For one of Ferenczi's basic theses was that if anger and hostility are allowed sufficient expression, confidence and love must at last take precedence.

Ferenczi, in preserving both his integrity and his friendship with Freud, created a shining example of his own most deeply felt precepts and beliefs. Though weakened by illness, he was still able to express, in his relation with his friend and teacher, the same self-searching and cherishing response which his richly loving nature gave to all his patients. This response, though tested throughout the years, was in neither case a matter of "technique." It arose because he was being quite simply himself; it was a full expression of his whole way of living, his fulfilled personality at the height of its maturity. It was the triumphant affirmation of his extraordinary capacity to give love.

PART I. Dynamic Undercurrents in Psychoanalysis

CHAPTER I

THE UNACKNOWLEDGED ELEMENT IN PSYCHOTHERAPEUTIC CURE

"PSYCHOANALYTIC 'cure' is in direct proportion to the cherishing love given by the psychoanalyst to the patient; the love which the psychoneurotic patient *needs*, not necessarily the love which he thinks he needs and therefore demands."[1] These words crystallize the revolutionary contribution of Sándor Ferenczi to psychoanalytic technique, the core of his final therapeutic approach. A kindred formulation occurs in his last paper, "Confusion of Tongues Between the Adult and the Child" (1932): "If *more love or love of a different kind from that which they need*, is forced upon the children in the stage of tenderness, it may lead to pathological consequences in the same way as the *frustration or withdrawal of love* . . ." (Italics in the original.)

This concept goes far beyond the usual psychoanalytic practice in technique, content, and emotional experience. It demands of the therapist a new and specific attitude toward healing: a determination to offer to the conscious and unconscious areas of the patient's personality the degree and kind of loving care for which he is in fact starving. The therapist thus creates an open-

[1] Quoted from personal discussions with Dr. Ferenczi in Budapest, 1931 and 1932. See also Chapter 4, "The Psychoanalyst's Response."

ing for the fullest possible use of all the equipment of the good psychoanalyst: technical skill, empathy, and the ability to interpret accurately the message from the unconscious. This message, as is well known, is presented by the patient in symptoms, dreams and phantasies, rationalizations, behavior, and in his emotional attitudes—whether outspoken or kept secret—toward the analyst and toward all persons of importance in his past and present relationships. Such attitudes represent a purposeful activity in the unconscious realm and are referred to as "transference phenomena." They are manifested in continual attempts to "transfer" to the analyst, and also to other persons, the characteristics, favorable and unfavorable, factual and imagined, of the significant personalities in the patient's childhood. Additional insight is gained by the discovery and understanding of (1) the patient's infantile traumatic experiences, (2) the confusion of mind and emotions which these experiences induced, and (3) the strange and enigmatic need of all neurotic sufferers to repeat in adult settings their early conflicts. This emotional reliving is carried out quite unconsciously with the hope of reaching thereby a permanent solution of the conflicts. It is technically known as the "repetition compulsion." Many months of intensive study are needed to disentangle these compulsive attitudes and behavior from the essential needs of the patient's inherent and erstwhile healthy personality.

Ferenczi insisted upon the ultimate rescue of the innate personality as essential. This had been neglected in the analytic type of therapy previously practiced. Synthesis was, to Ferenczi, an inevitable outcome of analysis; it should be encouraged and greeted with appreciation. Both processes could only be carried out in a cherishing atmosphere.

The offering of loving care cannot be given, either by parent or by psychotherapist, on demand or in answer to threat. It must be given freely and spontaneously as a genuinely felt emotional expression. And it must provide an environment of trust and confidence and hope, so that the neurotic sufferer can gradually unburden himself of his conscious and unconscious anxieties; of his shame and guilt; of his hostility and plans of vengeance; of his rejected longing to love; of all his deeply hidden secrets. It must provide the environment (no matter how absurd it may objectively appear) which is essential to growth, to the unfolding of individuality. In other words, the therapist must give to the patient a replica of the birthright of love which was denied him, as an infant or a growing child, but which, if granted, would have assured him full stature as an individual in his own right.

This thesis is extraordinarily difficult for the therapist to carry out successfully. For one thing, he is confronted in himself with his own character formation. In addition to this subjective difficulty, he is viewed by the patient, under the "transference," as an approximate duplicate of one or both parents. These portrayals may or may not contain elements accurately characteristic of the therapist. In any case, the patient, as if the portrayal were entirely factual, must be allowed the expression of his anxiety as he struggles with the therapist, in lieu of his parents, under the "repetition compulsion." Eventually the patient must be helped to form a realistic appraisal of the therapist's true personality. Therewith a new struggle arises on a contemporary basis; for the therapist is a concrete person, with his own biases and prejudices, his ideals and moral judgments, his failures and successes as a human being. Whatever welcome or unwelcome significance these facts may contribute, the therapeutic aspect must without exception be based on the genuine wish of the therapist to assist the patient to discover his true nature and to devote himself to its development. How is it possible for the therapist, a fallible human being, to cherish successfully the patient's innate temperament, so that it may be allowed full growth?

This is the crux of the psychoanalytic problem. It is, of course, useless to expect perfection in the relationship of therapist and patient. But, because of the therapeutic analysis which each psychoanalyst should have experienced in his own training, he is in a position to appreciate his patient's striving to regain his individuality, and to encourage him with tenderness and patience. This beneficent circumstance cannot occur unless the therapist, from the first interview, has taken cognizance of his emotional reaction to the possible future patient, and has felt drawn to him as a person who appeals to his sympathy and interest. He must begin to see in him attributes with which he himself, due to his particular personality, can cooperate successfully. He must sense an ability, both in himself and in the patient, to work well together, to mesh, in their mutual endeavor. Without these clear indications the analyst should refuse to begin the therapeutic treatment. For him to undertake the analytic procedure with a hostile or even an indifferent attitude toward the patient dooms their efforts to failure. In an atmosphere of mutual confidence and respect there is true hope of success.

As the treatment proceeds and nears completion the developing personality of the patient naturally may not fulfill all the analyst's hopes and expectations. This should not weaken the analyst's warm regard and respect for his patient. For the unfolding of a personality, whether congenial or uncongenial to the therapist, points to the growth of individuality and to increasing emotional maturity, the true goals of psychotherapy. Undeterred the therapist must allow the patient full sway in his development and must recognize and assist him in his right to determine his destiny. This frequently demands of the therapist a yielding of his own personal values and wishes, in favor of his patient.

The ability to yield to the patient's needs, in contrast to the attitudes of the patient's parents, is a gift of love, a welcome substitution for the love which the patient should have been given in childhood but which, under traumatic circumstances, was withdrawn. The patient now, by this yielding, is allowed to exercise his true growth potentialities and in this exercise to experience and value his therapist's deed of love. In response he learns to express, through his ripening significance as an individual, his own love and gratitude toward his therapist.

The need to be a loving person, a need that is basic to growth, is hereby given voice and gratification. At long last the patient senses the opportunity to be the person that he was born to be. The adventure of using his temperament in pursuit of maturity is thereby offered to him; and life gains meaning.

Thus, if Ferenczi was correct, it not only follows that the therapist cannot hope to be successful where a serious gap exists between the facets of his own individuality and that of the patient; it also follows that in the very process of helping to free the patient's selfhood the therapist too finds self-development and self-realization. The devoted surgeon may accept all comers in the area of his specialty. Not so the devoted psychoanalyst, for only mutually loving people will rejoice over each other's successes. In human relations motives are empty unless accompanied by the relevant emotions.

Giving to the neurotic patient the hope and the healing experience of love makes way for a mutually loving relationship. This train of emotional circumstance in psychotherapeutic treatment has not as yet been adequately acknowledged or valued by the various schools of psychoanalysis. Yet for Sándor Ferenczi this was the sure measure of successful psychoanalytic therapy, the constant aim of his lifelong research.

Chapter 2

THE TIRELESS SEARCH OF SÁNDOR FERENCZI

The following exposition of the basic psychoanalytic technique of Sándor Ferenczi is designed to stress and summarize the purely technical changes from the Freudian procedure which Ferenczi introduced and consolidated, and to outline their theoretical foundation. It was upon this practical application that he increasingly, as the years progressed, shed an aura of emotional warmth.

Ferenczi's brilliant imagination led him naturally to unexplored areas of research. This research, combined with his own special blend of tender sympathy, creative phantasy, and a keen sense of reality, enabled him to define clearly certain elements in the emotional struggle of human beings, and to bring fundamental improvement to the already well-established technical developments of psychoanalytic therapy.

Bases of Neuroses

In substance, Ferenczi's concepts of the bases of all neuroses did not differ widely from those of Freud. For purely therapeutic purposes, however, he described them as follows. There must have actually occurred in the childhood of the individual, probably very early in his childhood, one of three sets of circumstances: (1) a traumatic experience of great intensity, necessitating immediate repression; (2) a sequence of less intense traumatic experiences, which may or may not be wholly repressed; (3) a constant exposure to the highly emotional reactions, either sadistic or masochistic, of one or more adults, the memory of which is not entirely repressed. That these three types of experiences are inevitably of a sexual nature Ferenczi hesitated to assert. He was, however, convinced of their traumatic character. He also found them existing in different combinations and in differing degrees of emotional intensity.

In reaction to such an experience or experiences, the child must immediately establish an immunity, first negatively by some degree of repression, and then by a positive construction of protective devices which in the end determine, to a large extent, his personality. These devices protect him not only from his threatening external environment but from his own destructive impulses, which he tends to hold at least partially responsible for the traumatic experiences and which also, because of their intensity, threaten to destroy him himself.

These protections or defense mechanisms, initiated because of their self-protective use, tend automatically to increase out of all proportion to the need for them and to carry along with them an ever-growing anxiety, which in turn calls for further defense. This process in a full-blown neurosis is like a mature cancer, in that it threatens to occupy the entire life of the individual, ending finally in the death of the personality.

Bases of Therapeutic Technique

As a means of contending with the self-consuming system which all neuroses represent, Ferenczi formulated certain new therapeutic principles based on the fact that the components of the system were actual parts of the individual's life, of his living experience, of his emotional relation to other living beings. The therapeutic process, therefore, should center dynamically around the mutual relationship of analyst and patient. Emotions, being the activating properties of living, must form the instrument for the establishment and continuance of the relationship. In that vital situation the analyst's aim is to assist the patient to penetrate through the repressed and distorted memories of his life to the traumatic occurrence or sequence of occurrences which are at the root of the neurosis; then to aid him to face dramatically the trauma or traumatic series by reliving it emotionally, not in its original setting but as an actual part of the analytic situation. The ultimate benefit of having emotionally re-experienced these early crucial moments of his life in an adult environment in which he is protected by the presence and aid of his devoted analyst lies in the transformation of his fear of the overpowering passions within him into a new valuation of them as powerful assets.

Ferenczi's method of inducing this dynamic train of analytic experiences is based on the following three precepts.

1. An emotional relationship between analyst and patient must be allowed to form and must be constantly maintained. This is initiated in the relieving of the patient's anxiety by encouraging discussion of the analyst, discussion of the patient's most patent characteristics, and discussion of their mutual relation; and it is continued by maintaining a changing and highly charged situation between them, primarily by the use of dramatic dialogue rather than by the usual passive explanations and interpretations of the teacher-pupil relation. During this dialogue the analyst should, when occasion arises, express his own natural feelings to the patient in response. This serves to draw out a further expression of the patient's feeling. Such dramatic interplay must in no way be artificially induced; nor should any element of insincerity

or inappropriateness enter into it. It must arise spontaneously and naturally.

In continuing the drama, all is grist that comes to the mill: such as the analyst's eliciting criticism of his own personality; the attitude of friendly nearness to the patient, which makes unnecessary such artificial precautions as distance from the analytic couch, or furniture placed between analyst and patient; and the allowing of such freedoms as the acceptance of tokens of the patient's esteem and affection, meeting of analyst and patient outside of the analytic hour, when such a meeting comes about naturally, and any expression of kind friendliness on the analyst's part. The more natural and fearless the relationship on the part of the analyst, the more helpful it is to the patient. All that creates the atmosphere of parent and child being intimately together helps to maintain the dynamic relation that Ferenczi considered necessary.

Once we have established a relationship of mutual trust and confidence, we can safely leave to the patient's unconscious the shedding of the protective wrappings which shelter the wounded child. That shocked creature in each of us is like a magnet, full of potential power and exerting a tremendous pull towards any form of assistance that sets up a sympathetic vibration. Therefore, not only must we dispel the preliminary clouds of distrust and anxiety, but we must, as fellow human beings, accompany our patients through the shedding process.

2. Constant effort must be made by the analyst to pull the patient's emotional reactions back into the analytic setting, always bringing the analyst into the center by relating all associations and actions to himself. Although this occasionally creates resistance, it eventually strengthens the patient's belief in the endurance and sincerity of the analyst, and gradually concentrates the entire analytic drama upon this central figure. It seems

unnecessary to state that, in centering the patient's attention on the analysis itself, the analyst should give him no encouragement to neglect his outside responsibilities. These are not only extremely important in themselves, but also serve as a control, a scale of reality, against which the patient's reactions within the analysis can be measured. External responsibilities are the real objects which, when mirrored in the analytic process, tend to show distortion. To be able to calibrate these distorted images against the actual objects themselves is of great benefit.

3. In order to bring to the surface the critical dramatic moments of the analysis, care must be taken to avoid alleviating the emotional tension. Technical terms, although they may be reassuring to the analyst, break the current between the two individuals. Interpretative explanations also tend to clear the air, interrupting the strain of the situation, and should be sparingly used. They can, however, be occasionally thrown into the dialogue, arousing in the patient the feelings which at the actual time of the related experience had been necessarily repressed, and producing in him an increase in the tension of the particular moment. Throughout the treatment an effort is made to stimulate and maintain dramatic tension in proportion to the increasing strength and emotional health of the patient. This is for the purpose of cutting open the road to the deeply hidden cause of sickness, upon the secret existence of which the whole neurotic organization has been built. There is constant empirical proof that the anxiety which increases as the tension mounts is suddenly relieved after the climax and is followed temporarily by a healthy confidence and strength. This condition allows the entrance onto the analytic stage of new material and new anxieties, the latter, like the proverbial snowball, again growing disproportionately and inevitably towards a new crisis. Such a continual spiral motion functions like a rotating drill, cutting its way to

the center of the neurotic disturbance, seeking gradually and finally to relieve the dangerous pressure of the hidden passionate impulses.

The Six Stages of Psychoanalytic Treatment

To simplify the following illustrations of Ferenczi's therapeutic technique, it seems best to divide the treatment into six stages. Needless to say, this division is merely diagrammatic. In presenting these stages I hope to emphasize successfully the three technical principles already mentioned: that of a constantly maintained and thoroughly studied emotional relationship between analyst and patient; that of a dynamic concentration of the analytic drama upon this relationship and upon the figure of the analyst throughout the entire treatment; and that of the continual heightening of the patient's emotional tension until the original trauma or traumatic sequence shall have been exposed and explored.

FIRST STAGE OF TREATMENT

(The patient decides to be analyzed.)

The introduction of a suffering person to such an unfamiliar and frighteningly complicated course of therapy as psychoanalysis affords at the outset an opportunity for clearing away some of the most superficial symptoms of anxiety and, in proportion, for establishing sufficient trust in the analyst to enable the patient to undertake the treatment. Here the analyst's skill is almost entirely intuitive, as too much kindness or too much matter-of-factness may be equally inhibitive. One must be able to see immediately in the mannerisms of the prospective patient the general superficial protections with which he has equipped himself in dealing with a frightening world. And behind these externalized defenses one must sense the form of his inner need. At the first interviews the neurotic patient unwittingly presents to the analyst his central conflict, as in a nutshell. If it is then and there very carefully exposed to him in the words with which he himself, all unaware, has presented it, he is disarmed by the analyst's sensitivity. His own superficial defenses have not been able to mislead the analyst. The analyst seems to speak his own language if he can thus penetrate to the inner difficulty of which the patient himself is as yet unconscious. The analyst's immediate empathy relieves the patient of sufficient anxiety to allow him the confidence necessary to begin treatment.

Example: A young acquaintance of our family had been sent to me by his relatives, who knew of his incapacitating depressions. Although he was himself aware of his wish to be analyzed, he could not at first admit to me that he was thinking of such a step, but simply said that he wished to talk to me. We had several talks and I urged him to undertake an analysis, for I liked him, felt that I could help him, and hoped that he would come to me. He said that he would let me know of his decision in a month. Several months went by. A little later I met him in the street. During our greetings he said that he wished to see me very soon. A few weeks later he made an appointment, only to tell me that he had almost decided to go out West on a job, and so start life anew. I could see that, as a protection, he was unconsciously maintaining a kind of bluff and that in testing me he hoped to find some proof of my ability to sense the bluff and thus to help him. I accused him of treating me just as he had treated his various professors, his much older brother, and his father: expecting them to assume all responsibility for him and then making them powerless to use it to his advantage. I disarmed him by asserting that he had originally told his story to me in such a way that, if I had any kind thought for him, I should have to urge him to be analyzed, thus taking the initial responsibility upon myself. Afraid, however, to trust any show of kindness in me, he had tested me over and over again, always raising my hopes and dashing them, afraid that I should punish him by refusing to analyze him and hoping that I could stand the test.

The final proof came when he told me of his plan to go out West. As answer to this last threat he had expected more urging on my part, not a serious summing up of his uncertain behavior, which summary both frightened him and won him over. Unpleasant as he found my discovery of his motives, he was able to understand the significance of the former months of worried uncertainty and to acknowledge that underneath his proving of me was a great wish to trust someone sufficiently to accept her aid. It seemed that he could now have confidence in me because I had seen through his scheme without reproving him.

My exposure of his method of indirect attack made it possible for him to acknowledge his longing for a trusting, affectionate relationship, his fears that such a relationship could not exist for him, and his method of defense against recurring disappointment. It was now apparent to me that through our uncovering of his most evident protective mechanism we were at last beginning to build some slight foundation of mutual confidence. This was seen in the young man's emotional relief, his relaxation, and his definite plan to begin his analysis at once. The same battle would, of course, be fought over and over again as the analysis progressed, and of this I warned him. That warning in itself was a proof to him that I was willing to be the battleground. It increased his trust and made his superficial defenses less necessary.

SECOND STAGE OF TREATMENT

The patient becomes aware of his superficial mannerisms and habits, and discovers that he uses them to protect himself against frightening situations.

The early part of the treatment consists primarily in continuing what has been so tentatively accomplished in the first interview. By dramatic dialogue and the constant referring back to the analyst and to the analytic situation, an effort is made to break down the defense mechanisms and thereby to bring to light the material of the patient's inner conflict. Ferenczi recognized that the patient resists with all his power the coming to grips with his fears and longings in regard to his analyst. Instead, he attempts to attract the analyst's attention to the world outside and will go to great lengths in order to succeed in this, thereby allaying his own anxiety and falling back into the seeming security of his neurosis. Only by the analyst's tireless insistence on the immediate importance of the analytic relationship can the subject matter of his anxiety be brought into the open and the anxiety itself be admitted.

Example 1: This was illustrated in a language mannerism of a patient who at an early stage in his analysis discouraged me by constantly discussing very trivial circumstances of his everyday life, expressing little anxiety. Yet he was in analysis because of sexual impotence and inability to form successful social relationships. The analysis seemed to have reached a deadlock, nothing was happening, there was apparently no emotional tension in him. In an attempt to pull him back to the analytic center and to me, I drew his attention to the fact that he had lately begun to introduce each sentence with the phrase, "Well, I don't know," and very often threw into the context the phrase "You know." He was completely unaware of this habit but soon grew to realize how constantly he used these phrases and that in fact they meant just what they said. He was refusing to know or admit anything and was insisting on my taking the responsibility for all decisions, ideas, and feelings which were in reality his own. He would not take the consequences of them.

This discovery not only showed him intellectually how afraid he must be of the smallest responsibility but made him aware of an ardent unconscious wish that he were a girl with breasts and no penis. This wish he now expressed consciously, at the same time anxiously begging me to take care of him and not to expect anything of him, to help him get rid of the woman with whom he was then involved, and to protect him from further sexual affairs. He then admitted that he had feared that I, like his mother, would consider him incapable of competing with other men. In calling attention to his superficial mannerism I had awakened his anxiety and emotional tension in the present in regard to me.

Such evidences of anxiety should be immediately brought to the patient's notice—to his immediate discomfiture but to his eventual relief. Accompanying the anxious symptoms are the problems themselves, around which the anxiety centers. These now take the center of the stage, as will be seen in the next case.

Example 2: This patient greeted me on each of the first few mornings with an open and delightful smile, saying, "Well, how are *you*?" He then lay down stiffly, always in the same position in every detail, and remained quiet for ten or fifteen minutes. His only action was to moisten his dry lips with his tongue. Finally he spoke of some recent occurrence or thought, using stilted and intellectualized language, each word carefully chosen, his voice gentle, and with little expression of face. He was surprised to hear this description of himself and of the impression he made on me: that of being a frightened person, whose every move from his beaming smile of greeting to his careful speech and posture was calculated first of all to create a friendly atmosphere and then to keep it friendly, in order to forestall any chance of irritation on my part. Reacting to this description as to an attack, the patient threw out his chin. I drew his attention to this action, asking if I had irritated him. He then stretched his neck and rubbed his collar, and I remarked that he was trying to blame his collar instead of me. At this he blushed and quickly went on to some fresh topic, and I let him go. A little later in the hour he said that he always wore quiet clothing for fear of criticism from passers-by in the street. This remark, I told him, probably referred to me, as he undoubtedly felt that I had been criticizing him, and wished that I would "pass him by." I also said that I realized that such feelings must be difficult for him to acknowledge, adding that there were surely many things about me which he did not like. With difficulty he agreed that he hadn't liked either my noticing his irritation or my personal remarks about his chin and collar, for he knew that he had been angry with me and hadn't wanted me to know it. He also admitted that he had a bad temper and that his father had one, too. He had once been afraid that his father would kill his younger brother.

During the next few days of analysis he spoke often of his growing consciousness of the many mannerisms and habits which he had acquired in order to ensure for himself a non-irritating environment. He had recently asked some of his friends about this and they had said that they also had noticed these characteristics in him. As he became more aware of his superficial anxieties and his need to protect himself from them, he grew more able to admit the underlying anxieties—his childhood fear that his father would, through his cruelty, force his mother to have another child, and finally his fear of his own homosexuality. This latter was a difficult subject for him to broach. That so much material came, and came with appropriate feeling, during this first week of analysis, was due to his becoming conscious of his anxiety and of his anger through the discussions which I kept centered around himself and me. In this early stage of the treatment such discussions cannot be as dramatic in tone as they later become. But they can be actively directed by the analyst in order to prevent the patient's attention from wandering into paths of emotional escape, and in order to heighten the tension which threatens at every opportunity to decrease.

Owing to my stimulation, this patient became more and more anxious in regard to his feelings about me; but, simultaneously with the expression of his fears, he experienced added relief in finding that these personal discussions did not result in any danger to him, but, on the contrary, increased his confidence in me. He had had a chance to learn that my calling his attention to his mannerisms was not an act of hostile criticism, and that in telling me what he did not like about me he had not been misunderstood and hence punished by me. To have learned to let drop some of his defenses, to have dared to speak critically to another person, were to him entirely new and heart-warming experiences. He rewarded me for giving him this slight relief and security by giving me in exchange the present of very difficult and frightening material.

THIRD STAGE OF TREATMENT

The patient learns the emotional causes of his fears through examination of his character traits and through observation of his habits of behavior, in particular towards the analyst.

With the disappearance of the more superficial forms of anxiety and protection comes a new stage in the analytic process. The mechanisms that motivate the patient remain the same, but the subject matter of these mechanisms changes. In place of habits of personal appearance and action we now have to deal with character traits and the more serious problems and results of behavior.

As we make our way closer and closer into the heart of the

patient's neurosis, two dynamic processes seem to be activating the analysis.

1. The patient is driven to act out much more seriously, and frequently with some degree of danger to himself, his ever-present compulsion to test his environment. This he does in many different disguises. He tests his family, his old friends, and new friends. In all this activity outside of the analysis he is, of course, continuing to test his analyst. At such junctures the analyst must, with all his skill, attract the patient's attention and activity again to the analytic situation, the focal point of the therapeutic process. It is, however, unavoidable that new sets of emotional circumstances frequently appear for the first time as actions in the external world. Upon their appearance they should be immediately drawn into the analytic world. In the first interview and subsequently, we have seen this method of attack used in relation to superficial manners and habits. In this third stage, also, the same method must be applied in dealing with the patient's increasingly active tendencies. Each such occasion has similar earmarks and from it the analyst, and finally the patient also, learns the essential characteristics of the actual traumatic happenings of his early childhood.

2. In company with this more courageous and more frightening behavior, one senses a constant growth in self-confidence, a more healthy appearance, and a greater degree of trust in the analyst. As this more healthful side of the picture enlarges, more strength is also seen in the compulsive drive to push the analyst beyond his endurance. The resolution of such stormy conflicts is to some extent due to the analyst's open and honest expression of his own reactions to the patient. He may be tried and disheartened; he certainly dislikes many of the patient's characteristics. Such feelings the patient expects in the analyst, dreading at the same time lest he has really outraged him. If,

after the height of the storm, the analyst admits his discouragement or his irritation or his encouragement or admiration, as the case may be, the patient's fear of destruction is lessened. To find the analyst not unlike himself in human feelings increases his confidence and tends to assure him of the analyst's sympathy. Such a situation is different from any relationship that the patient has ever before experienced. To be sullen or angry day after day, to be allowed and encouraged to express that anger, to be received each of these days with constant and respectful care, to be told frankly and clearly but without anger the analyst's reactions to such occurrences, helps greatly to relieve the intense anxiety that has surrounded the patient since his earliest days and gives him the strength to continue the search for its original source. Not only is his anxiety relieved, but, in proportion to its relief, there is initiated a steady capacity to reach out from self-absorption, to sense in himself tender and deepening feelings for a person other than himself.

Example: As an example of this period of the treatment, when observation of the patient's superficial manners changes and becomes concentrated on his actual behavior, I will describe an hour with a young man who had been in analysis for three months. His first remarks had to do with a dream of the previous night, in which he had visited "an eye doctor," arriving at the doctor's office forty-five minutes late. In examining his eye the physician rubbed his finger around the eye many times, as the patient himself actually did almost continuously during his analytic hours. Finally the doctor suggested sending the patient to another doctor, whose name was confused in the patient's mind. After exclaiming over this "senseless dream," the young man told me that at last over the week-end he had succeeded in the hitherto difficult task of enjoying a social evening with friends; but that when they wished him to go with them to a dance the following evening, he had felt that there were many reasons why he could not accept, and afterwards he had realized that they were only pretexts and regretted not accompanying his friends. His roommates had left him alone the next afternoon and he had taken the occasion to masturbate, but only "in the spirit of getting it over with." He had lately been worrying about the problem of finding a job and had decided not to follow my suggestion but to hunt for one at once. I had previously tentatively suggested that with his strong resistance to accomplishing his college work, it might be informing to see for a while how he would react to no schedule and no job.

Throughout this analytic hour the patient had been restless, dissatisfied, and anxious, with perspiring hands. I brought to his attention the fact that these symptoms, together with the restless and unsatisfying activity of the week-end, had been dramatized in the dream, and that in all three forms he was showing his dissatisfaction with me, his "I-doctor," and was expressing some impulse to find another analyst. He seemed, indeed, to be making a laughing stock of me and to be telling me that my wish, as he interpreted it, to encourage him to be social, also to masturbate, and to enjoy himself instead of seriously undertaking a job, would lead to utter confusion for him.

This interpretation was exceedingly distressing to him; he felt that he was being accused of making a fool of me. I further accused him of attacking me, not directly in angry words, but indirectly in his dream and actions, which showed in dramatic form his complaint of the poor results afforded by my treatment. I told him that it was evident that he must be greatly irritated with me for trying to upset his lifelong compulsive habits. At my words he was torn between his fear of losing these habits, his anger with me for disturbing them, and, paradoxically, his relief that someone had at last discovered his destructive wishes, thus making them powerless, and was not deterred by them. Tears came into his eyes and he expressed his severe struggle in saying: "All I can say is that I don't like you less for what you've just shown me. I don't as yet seem able to admit that I really like you more."

That I showed him what a potential danger I seemed to him in my guise as his helper, and that I did not blame him for making a fool of me in retaliation, relieved him of some anxiety and hence brought slight and ambivalent feelings of tenderness to the surface. This analytic hour represented an unconscious attempt on the patient's part to deal with his struggle for independence against his upbringing. The attempt was dramatized in the emotionalized situation between analyst and patient. In order to maintain this dramatic tension, what interpretations I had made had not referred in any way to his past experience but were entirely concerned with us and with the situation between us. This was growing more and more acute. He felt intensely his resentment against me for confusing him with my tempting suggestions to lay aside his strict self-discipline and to enjoy himself. He was also frightened at his anger with me. Here there was brought into the analytic experience a duplicate of the frightening relation of father and son. That relationship was now actually relived but with a different outcome. To his surprise, this son now found that he would not be harmed if he dared to express both his rebellious feelings against me and his fear of thus expressing them.

Such a slight crisis is an example on a small scale of the ultimate crisis towards which the patient was making his way. It was for him, however, an occurrence of some magnitude; particularly so because, existing in the immediate present and involving a person of increasing value to him, it had to be faced and could not be avoided. This was symbolized by a dream in which he stood at the end of a high diving board trying to find the courage to dive into a pool far below, where other swimmers, who had just dived successfully, were playing a delightful game. He felt that his future security and happiness were at stake. He was caught between his feelings of rebellious anger with me and an increasing need for me.

The opportunity of re-experiencing the disastrous moments of his childhood not only shows the patient, through a highly emotionalized medium, the contents of his unconscious life, but also helps him to realize, through his own immediate and imperative personal struggle with the analyst, that his ingrained fears are no longer insoluble, that in the analysis they can again be felt directly in reaction to an actual situation and this without a destructive result. This relief from anxiety gives rise to the emotional strength to face the next ordeal.

FOURTH STAGE OF TREATMENT

The patient admits the hopeless failure of his neurotic protections against anxiety and, as a result, openly attempts a direct struggle against the threat of destruction which the analyst seems to him to represent.

Through long months of analysis the patient is gradually becoming more and more enmeshed in a maze of his own making. Wherever he turns, whether into contemporary situations outside the analysis or into memories of his childhood, he is constantly confronted with the same causes for anxiety, the same defenses against anxiety, and the same sterile results of these defenses. Here again, Ferenczi's method of active participation on the analyst's part in the emotional turmoil is used to keep the patient constantly aware of the hopelessness and failure of his former methods of protection and escape. He does not know where to turn; and there results a time of great despair. With this despair the emotional tension attains a high level. This the analyst should continually focus on himself. The success of this technique lies, to a great extent, in the fact that the analyst is working in cooperation with the patient's unconscious, and therefore, in the patient's eyes, is working against him. This cooperation with the unconscious is a powerful tool and provides the impetus which drives the patient even more intently and angrily towards the very figure whose purpose in his life is to bring him to health. That this figure seems instead to have successfully destroyed even the little that he had so carefully constructed in his neurosis, infuriates him; and he, in turn, is confronted with the impulse to destroy him. Here we see approaching the great conflict of the analysis, the counterpart of the early and equally terrifying original trauma. If health is now to be regained, the analytic struggle must result in the final breaking down of the strong defenses against the analyst, in the courageous, direct emotional attack against him and its successful outcome, and in the ultimate discovery that in this victory he becomes a valiant, carefree person in his own right.

Example: A case after several years of analysis may now be in point. This young man had from birth been a continual disappointment to his family and to all his friends. As his parents had wanted only daughters, he was at birth given over to a governess, remaining always the ugly duckling of the family, while his sister was treated as a beautiful swan. As a result, his life was devoted to proving himself the prey of all about him, particularly in his adulthood the prey of women of his sister's age. This, of course, brought great unhappiness and ruin to others besides himself. His external hardness of manner, combined with a hypersensitive show of pride, in which the ugly duckling masqueraded as a man of the world, were at first the prevailing signs of his anxiety. He had developed great skill in apparent self-possession and indifference. Many months of analysis passed before he dared to throw off these protections and could allow himself to feel the despair of being an unloved person. Probably this new courage was due to the fact that, no matter how he acted or how cruel he seemed, I remained faithful and trusting. I could, however, have little affection for such an unlovable person. This I told him. But at least he was endured; and, more than that, he learned that I was earnestly endeavoring to help him. He found that he could distress me and greatly discourage me, even to the extent of admissions on my part that perhaps, after all, there was no hope of his complete recovery. Yet I stood by him and worked with him wholeheartedly. No one had ever done this much for him before; and gradually he had the courage to lay aside his useless, cruel brittleness and be a sad, confused, and very lonely child. This very sincerity brought him friends and developed in him a great capacity for loyal devotion. His violent envy and destructive anger towards women slowly eased, as his belief in his own integrity and in his capacity for devotion strengthened. He became too valuable to himself to be any longer a despised duckling.

As he timidly began to discard his defense against the other sex and to try to value women for themselves and for his happiness, instead of as instruments of disaster, an early form of anxiety returned. He became exaggeratedly sensitive to criticism. His old brittleness and sullenness of manner were resumed. This attitude became increasingly directed at me and it seemed probable that, in order to rid himself of his anger against women in general, he was preparing to shift the battlefront again to the analysis. This had, of course, occurred at frequent intervals throughout the treatment. On this occasion, however, the emotional setup had a different ring to it. There was now a hollowness in his reactions to the outside world. By way of the analysis, he was very evidently beginning justifiably to blame his mother, rather than his sister, for his long life of disaster. His emotional strength seemed to me sufficiently great for me to allow him his head, and then to stand by to watch him find his own method of control.

This resulted in my keeping almost entirely silent for a period of many weeks. At the beginning of this period of silence he had early in the hour asked me a question, not from interest in the answer but to avoid a momentary hurt. I had not replied. This had further hurt his pride and he had become sullen. The remainder of the hour was spent in silence on both our parts. His tendency the following day was to overlook this situation between us. In order to keep him centered in the analytic field, I reacted with continued silence to his attempts to change the emotional tone. In so doing I was able to maintain the tension of the previous day. His increasing anxiety then manifested itself in his redoubled sensitivity. His anger became intense, and with it the fear of unloosing it and doing some real damage to me. His only refuge was in maintaining a sullen, passive attitude. At the end of each hour I let him go out of the door without a word from me to relieve the tension. The following two weeks were almost entirely spent in silence, except for the relating of his dreams at the beginning of each hour. These dreams were revealing as evidences of his intense conflict. He had sufficient insight to make it unnecessary for me to assist him in their interpretation. Such an act on my part would have been seized upon by him as a friendly generosity and thus would have immediately relieved the tension between us. Nor did I at this juncture feel generously towards him. The insistent urge at last to express his aggressiveness towards me directly, his terror of the consequences, his lifelong defensive attitude of sullen withdrawal from every irritating situation, his retention of this protection to which he was accustomed, his inability to see any way out of the dilemma —all of this struggle, together with a slowly developing determination to work his way through to the finish, was represented in a series of dreams, of which I give below some fragmentary excerpts.

1. "He popped up from behind a bush and shot at me. I rushed at him and shook him and scolded him. Afterward I felt sorry I'd done it."

2. "A dreadful nightmare . . . that I hit a man over the head. He turned on me and chased me. Suddenly there were horrible explosions. Pieces of rock and iron pipes were flying through the air. . . . I was terribly frightened."

3. "I was driving my car. I came round a corner and there were three cars that had run into each other. There was no way to avoid them. I just had to run up on them. I was furious. . . . I knew in my dream that it was about the analysis and now I see how afraid I am that I will have to attack you—that there's no way out of it. I wish I could see some way out!"

4. "A map was spread out on the floor and I pointed to the places where I had been, and then showed Billy where we would have to fly, across a desert, and told him that in the middle there was a hidden city. You couldn't see it on the map, but I knew it was there. Billy was to pilot the airplane and he said that he wouldn't fly over the desert. But I was determined to go. Then we were in the plane above the desert and I saw the city and showed it to him and proved that I was right."

In these dreams my patient expressed his mounting anxiety, his fear of unexpected anger on my part, his fear of an uncontrolled outburst against me on his part, and the despair of helplessness and hopelessness in himself. In the last dream—which he characterized as "made to order"—he finally admitted to himself and to me that he *did* know a way out of his impasse with me; and that he would find it. This was a ray of hope for us both.

The way in which dreams reveal not only our fears and hopes but also our search for solutions was crystallized by Ferenczi in a brief note, dated March 26, 1931: "Thus instead of 'the dream is a wish fulfillment' a more complete definition of the dream function would be: every dream, even an unpleasurable one, is an attempt at a better mastery and settling of traumatic experience, so to speak, in the sense of an *esprit d'escalier* which is made easier in most dreams because of the diminution of the critical faculty and the predominance of the pleasure principle."[1]

My patient's dreams had occurred over a period of five weeks, during which time I had maintained an almost complete silence. He was in great conflict with himself. I was an onlooker, waiting and ready to prevent him from harming himself or me, if such an impulse arose. He used me during these weeks as material for his struggle; built up and pulled down many phantasies of my iniquity; was constantly complaining of my unfriendliness, untrustworthiness, of my variable treatment of him, of my stubborn insistence on having my own way. All of these characteristics were typical of his own mother. He insisted that he would win out against me, even if it should mean his giving up the analytic treatment, and hence not gaining his health. As a final threat, he threatened to kill himself. Many analytic hours were spent by him buried in a blanket, lost in silence. A tremendous struggle was being enacted each day during his hour. Gradually my own endurance was being worn down and I grew aware of my increasing anxiety on his behalf. The day came when I myself could no longer stand the tension. I feared that he could not win the battle. I found that I must confess that he had more power than I; that I was too weak to stand his constant silent sullenness as an indirect method of attacking me; that I was nonplussed and knew no further way of helping him; that although a future victory over himself was of great moment to

[1] *Esprit d'escalier,* "staircase wit," comprises the perfect repartee that we always think up too late, walking downstairs *after* leaving the party.

me, I was now terribly disheartened. My admissions of defeat, of course, proved to him my affectionate concern and also his superior strength, and for a moment pleased him. Almost immediately, however, he began again to accuse me, this time directly and justifiably. By my confession, by my weakness, I had deprived him of a battlefield. Why hadn't I let him alone, why was I an analyst if I was so weak? For the rest of the hour he maintained an honest and direct attack on me. During the next week came the following dreams.

5. "I dreamed that I was masturbating, but kept being interrupted and I was frantic. I went from place to place, trying to find some place where I could be alone, but I was always interrupted."

6. "A dream about Tommy. I was to go to one small town and he to another. When he arrived, he was to telephone me and I was to drive over to him. I went to my town, and waited and waited. No word! So I finally went over to his town and there he was, dead drunk. I was furious and raged at him. But I realized that it would do no good, I couldn't change him, so I shut up and went back to my town."

The following dialogue took place between us as the result of this last dream:

P. "I know that dream has to do with you and me. First of all, Tommy is you and that's the way I've felt these last six weeks about you. Also in the dream you are me, and I am Tommy. You can't change me, no matter how hard you try. And yet I know there is a point in my changing; and instead of shutting up, I should really face you when you infuriate me."

A. "What could that point be?"

P. "Well, I'd be more honest. I would really be expressing my feelings. But I don't dare!"

A. "Why not?"

P. "If I'd done that with Tommy I'd have lost him."

A. "So you think I couldn't stand it?"

P. "If I broke your favorite picture or gashed your face with the ashtray, you might very well say that you were through with me; that I could tell you my anger but you weren't going to have me around destroying things. That's what I'm afraid I will do."

A. "And if I said that?"

P. "Well, I'd lose you and I need you. You're all I've got!"

A. "All right. What if I did turn you out?"

P. "I'd be furious and I'd say to myself that you weren't any good anyway."

A. "But you've just said that I was important to you, that I was all you had."

P. "Yes, but I'd be too proud to acknowledge it and anyway I can get along the way I am, even though I am mad all the time, even though that makes me unhappy and despairing. I'm used to it and know how to deal with it."

A. "If I'm so valuable to you, why should you let me go so easily?"

P. "But I've already lost you."

A. "Only if you really killed me, would I be lost. If I'm in the world and you're in the world, there's always the chance of getting me back again."

P. "I don't see how. I could try to come back here again. But, of course, I'd have to admit that I was glad I'd finally lost my temper at you, that I'd finally told you my real feelings, and that it was the best feeling I'd ever had."

A. "Of course."

P. "But then you'd hurt my feelings again. You might say that even if I had been honest, you couldn't have me around."

A. "I'd throw you out again?"

P. "Yes, and I'd be furious; and I'd never come back."

A. "I'd still be lost to you. But, you know, I'd still be here."

P. "I don't see any way of getting you back. I might kill myself."

A. "Then you would surely lose me."

P. "Or get very sick. No, I can't see any way. I'd be too proud to let myself know that I had to have you."

A. "But you're an ingenious person. You can imagine some way of getting me back, even if you've never experienced it."

P. "I might get sick with brain fever."

A. "Why that?"

P. "Because I love you so. *There,* that's it. How did that feeling ever come out? It came out without my knowing it. But how could I ever show you that I love you if I also get furious with you? I'd want you to love me. I might discover a cure for cancer."

A. "Why should that make me love you?"

P. "I'd be admirable."

A. "But that doesn't mean you'd be lovable."

P. "I could pretend to be lovable."

A. "But I'd probably see through that and not like it."

P. "I don't know how to be really lovable. And yet I can be such good friends with the stenographer or the elevator boy; lose my temper at them and still be good friends."

A. "Perhaps that's because it doesn't really matter if you lose them. It does matter if you lose me."

P. "What the hell! Then I wouldn't have this damned mess on my hands!"

The hour ended here, and without relief in the patient's tension.

In the dreams is seen a slow acceptance of his knowledge that he must now face me in whatever guise I might seem to him to be at the moment. All the feelings of fury, impatience, jealousy, and envy, which had been so disastrous in his relations with others, had lately seemed to direct themselves at me. He was in constant fear of physically destroying me and so proving to others the reality of the insanity which he imagined they suspected in him. He was also afraid of being himself physically and mentally destroyed by his overwhelming force of feeling. These fears were in conflict with his belief in my sincere wish to help him to get well. There then arose in him the stubborn refusal to give in to me, the refusal to admit the success of my analytic treatment by getting well. It would be better not to improve in health and so to beat me at my own game. He could manage, now that he was somewhat better. He could get along, and his present state was a familiar one. To make the plunge, to fly over the desert, even if it might possibly bring him real recovery and happiness, might on the other hand end in complete disaster. Better to stay as he was than risk failure, especially as in staying as he was he remained in power over me. This battle was accompanied by feelings of great despair. His life outside the analysis was sterile, meaningless, and automatic. He tried not to think of me or of his analysis and took refuge in his old defenses, realizing at the same time that they held no protection for him. This was extremely wearing to both him and me. But he soon learned that my admission of defeat was of no help to him, was in reality a hindrance, as it lessened the tension of his struggle. He alone must fight the battle and win it. With this realization, these questions arose at last in his phantasy: Does hatred preclude love? Might not winning the fight be a way of winning my affection, even if it necessarily involved the expression in words of his direct and passionate aggressiveness towards me?

FIFTH STAGE OF TREATMENT

The patient safely relives the traumatic experiences of his early childhood through direct, crucial, and aggressive emotional conflict with the analyst.

In the previously quoted hour we see the patient contemplating what he has always feared might happen to him. He feared that he might violently and destructively express his feelings, most particularly his hatred, in such a way that he would lose all that meant security to him. Gradually during his analysis he has learned to realize his fears of this possibility and, gathering his strength, has determined to discover whether, if he dares to feel the aggressiveness which has become increasingly directed at his analyst, he will actually suffer the destruction that has always hauntingly threatened his life. This attempt he can dare to make because, through his constant testing of the analyst, he has gained considerable trust in him. He now knows that, if he should allow himself to feel the fury of anger or of love that seems to possess him, he may gain immeasurably and may find a new health. If he fails, life can be no worse than it has always been. There is really no choice of action, for his former neurotic weapons have become valueless. Nevertheless, many months of hesitation pass. The pros and cons, dramatized emotionally and in behavior, seem to be revolving in the patient's unconscious, as he metaphorically girds up his loins to do battle, anticipating his own active role as antagonist. The analyst watches the preparation of the battlefield, and aids by refusing to let the patient's attention wander elsewhere. As we have seen, dreams are invaluable in estimating the progress of these preparations, and the directions which they are taking. They are also most important prognostic signs. At the approach of the final crisis of the analysis, they tend to recapitulate symbolically the actual traumatic occurrences of early childhood. This recapitulation may possibly form the stimulus which tips the balance in favor of succumbing in the analysis to the reliving of the trauma.

Example: The following series of dreams and associations occurred in the third and final year of analysis of a woman patient suffering from deep depressions. In them we see an outline of the constantly shocking early relationship between the mother and this child, and the child's reaction to this relationship. Increasingly evident is her eventual unconscious determination in the analysis to break through the vicious circle of her neurotic protections against the traumatic experiences and, by direct aggressive expression against the analyst, to fight for her independence and integrity and to regain the happy temperament which she grew to believe was hers by nature.

1. "I went into a room where there was a little girl. She was my little girl. On the plaster wall there was a fuse-box and all around it some child had stuck her fingers in the soft plaster, so that there were holes. It looked terribly messy. I knew that it was this little child who had done it and I scolded her and told her that she must never do it again. Then I had to go out of the room for a while.

"I came back and all around the fuse-box in designs were nails, copper and brass nails, very shiny. The little girl was sitting on the floor looking up at this, and over by the window was an older girl. I was furious that the little girl had done this to the wall after I had told her not to. I picked her up and beat her till she was just a little mass of white clothes, and threw her into the corner of the room where she lay like a heap of old rags."

Associations: "Mother always said that she never spanked me. The other children had been spanked but I never had been. The little child was myself. B., my sister, was sitting by the window, watching Mother spank me. B. knew that she herself had made the holes for mischief. The little child was too young to drive all those nails in, in designs, herself. B. had betrayed me although I had always worshiped and adored her. Perhaps I had called to Mother for help if B. had teased me. Mother came in and, instead of helping me, fell upon me in a fury, because she thought that I had done what she had already told me not to do. I can feel myself to be that pile of white clothes—crushed and almost destroyed—and the two people whom I had counted on, loved and adored, had betrayed me. Since then there has always been a conspiracy to keep up the fiction that I had never been spanked, because the one time that I *was* spanked, Mother almost killed me and didn't want to remember that. I didn't want to remember it either, because it stood for the moment when I lost everything. And B. didn't want to remember it, because she was guilty of letting me be punished for her, letting me be almost killed. So we have all been living the lie that I was never spanked."

In this dream and associations, we have perhaps a recounting of an actual very early trauma, before the patient could talk. She remembered that in her later childhood her mother had often comforted her when she had been hurt, had taken her on her lap and dried her tears; but this time, she had fallen upon her, "like an avalanche," and had beaten her until she was limp. Then, leaving her in the corner of the room, she had deserted her. For some time after this occurrence the patient never left her mother's skirts and in so doing assisted in establishing another fiction, that of being a model child who never did anything wrong. A most important element in this dream is the identification of the patient with her mother, "identification with the enemy,"[2] and the clear picture that is given of the moment in her life when, through this identification, she attempted to destroy a part of her own personality. "I beat her until she was just a little mass of white clothes."

[2] This role, generally assumed in neurotic organization, is specifically described by Clara Thompson, M.D., in a paper, "Identification with the Enemy and Loss of the Sense of Self," *Psychoanalytic Quarterly*, Vol. IX, 1940.

2. "A set of short dreams, all vague and as if I were a ghost in a haze, returning to visit the rooms and people whom I had loved and where I had lived."

(a) "In a bed with lots of starched, long, lacy petticoats. I felt smothered by them and a little curious of what was underneath them."

Associations: "The long period of sitting at Mother's skirts. I was dead then, hypnotized, drugged. The instinctive wishes were there but hazy as in a dream, foggy."

(b) "I was going to a dancing party and wanted a gardenia to wear. I went to a greenhouse to buy one but the man said that the gardenias were too far away for him to go and get one. Instead he offered me a china vase with pale blue, stiff little flowers growing in it, very artificial and not what I wanted at all. I took it."

(c) "In Maine, very beautiful weather, lovely scenery, spring. Good to be alive! You were with me. I told you of some lovely sugar maples that we could tap, for the sap was now running, and it would be such fun to make sugar. We started out so happy and gay, when someone called me from the house. A lot of businesslike, efficient girls were in the kitchen packing up to leave. One of them told me that I must fix the stove and put some cellophane over a hole on the side of the stove. I didn't want to do it or to cook, or to stay in the house; but I knew that I had to."

This second set of dreams continues to depict "the dutiful child" sitting always at her mother's skirts. The memories of this part of her life had been brought to the analysis during the first year and we knew thoroughly all the details. The child had sat by her mother for hours on end, afraid to move, afraid of her teasing sister; and, fearful that she might be scolded by her mother, she had watched her mother's every move, learning how to identify herself with her. Again a fiction sprang up in the family. There are letters written by the mother telling of little Mary's angelic disposition, how changed she was, how quiet and good, and how devoted. "She doesn't leave my side for a minute and sits by my skirts for hours doing nothing at all." These dreams, beginning with quantities of stiff, starched petticoats and a china vase of stiff, artificial flowers, give symbolically and very accurately the thoughts that must have run through the child's mind as she sat so quietly by her mother's skirts. The little girl did not dare to breathe her wonderings. All she dared be was a ghost, visiting the places where she had been happy, looking at those whom she had loved and lost, not daring to be alive, nor to remember what had occurred before she had been so cruelly beaten. "Hazy," "foggy," "like a ghost" are her associations to these dreams and we see that, although she knew what she wished to do, the slightest hindrance or wish from another person controlled her actions.

Here we have the continuance of the original repression. It is well installed, and the failing child has become a little ghost allowed to wander at will through all the childhood haunts but warned by some dim dreamlike memory never to dare to come alive again. This spectral existence at her mother's feet, protected from all harm and conscious fear, has the aspect of a hypnotic trance. This living death, like all repression, existed parasitically on the strength of the phantasy "as if . . . ." "I am acting as if I were alive, as if I had never lived before. My other life was a lie. It didn't happen." The last dream of the series, however, is full of hope that somehow she may feel happiness again. It forewarned me of her coming attempt to bridge the gap between her present analytic situation and her earliest and happy infancy. She wished me to accompany her on the adventure. But before we could "go out into the woods to tap the sugar maples" she herself must accomplish a difficult and trying piece of work.

The final dream occurred several weeks later when the patient was ill with influenza.

3. "I dreamed of a whole pile of old clothes made of small bundles of old clothes. The whole bundle was I. It looked the way a bundle does when you hold your arms out and hang clothes on them, entirely limp, hanging there, even more relaxed than a baby who is asleep. It seemed like a baby that had lost consciousness completely."

Associations: "I know now exactly how I felt before the first terrible punishment happened. I can remember the feeling and I've never felt it since. I can see that I've always been trying to get it back. Mother wrote in her letters that I always 'danced along' when I first began to walk, that I never just walked. I was so full of life and energy and joy, of a strong passionate feeling of loving. Such feeling is always aggressive. It is sheer passionate feeling with no differentiation of love and hate. In that dancing, happy mood of strong feeling, I may have lost my balance and fallen down. It would not have been my fault at all, someone might have tripped me—B., in teasing me. Or I stumbled because I was just learning to walk. I hurt myself, skinned and bruised my knees. Then, instead of being picked up and loved and encouraged back to self-confidence and high spirits, Mother shook me and scolded me and was angry because I hurt myself and tore my dress. I have often seen mothers and nurses treat children that way. I was so outraged at being scolded and even more hurt, when I was already in pain from my bruises, that I tried to pull away from her hands and arms, tried so hard that I kicked and screamed. She held me tight and I began to feel a frenzy of hatred. Before that, even after I had fallen down, I had been happy, in loving her so passionately and wholeheartedly. Suddenly, with her anger and her restraint of me, hate came into my heart. Then she must have caught me and beaten me and beaten me, until in self-defense I lost all sense of where I was. When I came to, I was in the same house, with the same people, but everything in me was entirely different. I had died as the passionate, strongly feeling, dancing child. I was a ghost, and from then on, I felt like slimy, gray, nasty spit."

In the third dream and its associations, no new material is found. We are, however, led back by the symbol of "old clothes" to the first dream of all, and find that during the three groups of dreams, covering a period of six weeks in the third year of analysis, not only have memories of an infantile trauma been reconstructed, but the memory has been recovered of a sense of well-being, of joy, and of a passionate happiness in loving that can be with difficulty reconciled with the patient's life as she had hitherto described it. This last memory, when once reawakened by the emotional stimulation of the third dream and its associations, became so ingrained in the patient's consciousness that her one ardent desire was to re-experience this condition. This, she felt sure, was her true nature, her birthright. From it she had been driven by a succession of shocks and losses that had necessitated the primal repression, its maintenance, and its fortification by means of later repressions.

During several weeks after these dreams, I could sense the gradual approach of an attempt to recover, as an actual experience with me, the complete memory of the traumatic event and of what her life had previously been. She seemed to realize that only by unreeling the film backwards could she get to the other side of the trauma, to her real nature, to the happy dancing little girl. It was as if, all unaware, she were preparing herself and at the same time relaxing her neurotic defenses. The angry, ardent side of her personality was growing in proportion to her ability to entrust herself to my care. At this stage of the analysis, she reminded me of a butterfly within the chrysalis. As the chrysalis becomes more and more weakened and brittle, the butterfly within slowly comes to life, grows in vitality, and fearfully pushes its way out into the light. Perhaps the insect at such a moment feels the sense of shock and apprehension that overcame my patient during two particular analytic hours when she finally emerged from the crisis and realized the uncontrollable impulse that had but a moment before held her in its sway.

As a result of the slight glimpse aroused by the third dream into her earliest and apparently joyful infancy, she grew more aware of the frustrations and deprivations that now separated her from the happy state of mind that had been recalled. Her behavior to me became increasingly that of a passionate imprisoned child. The situation in her own life, as well as that of the analysis, contrived to repeat almost in duplicate that of her childhood. Whatever she desired seemed to be just beyond her reach. She became very restless and very eager to escape from her immediate and excessively frustrating environment. An opportunity offered itself in an invitation to visit one of her children. She rather fearfully asked me if she might stay longer than a week end, in case she found she was capable of enjoying herself. I encouraged her to do this. She stayed five days, surprised to find herself happy and carefree.

Upon her return to the analysis, however, the hopelessness which had increased to an almost overwhelming extent through the past few months again enshrouded her. I could see in her daily reactions to me, in her fears and impulsive wishes, and in her timid attempts to break through the restraints that I represented, the duplication of the days at her mother's skirts. This frame of mind became increasingly intense after her trip. As I constantly confronted her with her slavery to me, she became more and more infuriated with me, her slave driver; but she nevertheless begged me to let her come to me at any time that she felt her uncontrollable reactions threatening her. This I promised. My cooperation with her deeply repressed impulses helped to allay her intense fears. The child that had sat at her mother's feet had unconsciously learned to keep in check her impatient and angry feelings by means of an unattached anxiety, which had arisen from the forgotten suffering at her mother's hands. For her to allow these angry impulses expression she needed a safe and tender mother. Only by very gradual and frightening tests could she believe that I might be such a person. In many analytic periods she tested and proved my sincerity, my patience, and my self-control. At the same time she became increasingly importunate, angry at the deprivations of her reality situation and overwhelmed by an unbearable longing for a safe and tender relationship with me. Finally, after an exceedingly stormy analytic hour, she telephoned and asked to come to me again, saying that she could control herself no longer. At the end of a period of two hours of intense agony, of complaints and anger and despair, long periods of hysterical sobbing and cries of woe, she cried herself quietly to sleep in my arms. In the interval before her next analytic hour she realized that she had, during those two hours, been possessed by an emotional state which had lacked all conscious control, that for moments at a time she had not known what she was saying or doing. To awaken and find herself safe, and to find that I had kept my word that I would protect her, gave her the courage in herself and faith in me to continue in her willingness to expose herself to such experiences.

This occurrence brought on a period of several weeks of nursing memories and reconstructions of her infancy. She happened at this very time to learn from an external source that three weeks after her birth her mother had, for a few months, sent her each day to a friend who also had a newborn baby, to be given supplementary nursings. In my patient's mind this necessity seemed to be due to some fault of her own. Stimulated by this distasteful information, the actual deprivations of her present situation assumed an aspect beyond endurance to her. She became more and more flooded with anger. She was filled with furious passions throughout her waking hours, occasionally venting her rage in destructive tantrums in her own home. I realized the danger of a physical attack on me and questioned whether this could be prevented without losing the therapeutic value of such a reliving. I believed, however, that her greatly improved mental health, her increasing self-confidence, and her admitted need of me would tip the scales in favor of a successful outcome of her present conflict.

Here the question of the diagnosis of the patient's illness is of extreme importance, as it is to a less degree throughout the treatment. If the patient is a borderline case and if there is, therefore, a chance of his seeking refuge in a psychosis, it is necessary, through the entire therapeutic process, to watch assiduously and sensitively the level of emotional tension, to relieve it when necessity demands, and not to allow the patient to run any risk whatever of succumbing to such a complete emotional seizure as was allowed in the case of the psychoneurotic patient here described. In a borderline patient one cannot depend on the normal self-protective element of fear which, like pain in organic illness, acts as a warning to the individual to pursue no further his present course of action. This protective mechanism of normal fear must be distinguished from neurotic anxiety. It is not without real cause and can be counted upon to interrupt at the vital moment and to prevent the consummation of an irrevocable destructive act. There is experienced, in such a seizure as I am here describing, the almost complete yielding to an overwhelming impulse and also the sure rescue by fear before actual harm has been done. This rescuing element functions more and more effectively as the neurotic patient grows in mental health and in the consciousness of his integrity and emotional strength. Such a condition had in this case been achieved, and the moment had arrived for me to allow her the freedom to act which she was unconsciously struggling to obtain.

Finally, in one of her analytic hours, I found myself obliged to refuse an invitation to lunch with her. Suddenly she threw herself at me, screaming out her angry wish to kill me. I put my arms around her and we knelt together by the couch, she sobbingly asking me if she had hurt me, telling me that I should never have let her reach that point of lost control and that it was my fault, and not hers. Gradually she began to realize that she had experienced the power of an instinctive impulse in its direct expression and had repeated in this temper tantrum the kind of emotional seizure which she had felt as a child and which she had described in her associations to the third dream.

For the next few weeks she expressed in words and mood the probable reactions of her mother to her original tantrum, and of herself towards her mother. First she would denounce her own furious impulses, feel ashamed of them, and try to prove that they brought her scorn and ill-treatment from others. In actuality she imagined herself openly shunned by her nearest friends. Then she would denounce me for being the occasion of the tantrum, saying that I, and not she, was responsible for it. Slowly these reactions against her angry impulses and their expression weakened. She realized that her passionate and almost unconscious rage had had no ill effects; nor had it changed the frustrating facts of her circumstances. Again came periods of complaint and anger, but the anger came more fully and openly in words than she had ever before allowed herself, and did not again take the form of direct physical attack.

In time, these reactions were replaced by wonder that she remained unpunished by me and that she had actually harmed no one and was herself unharmed. She was astonished at having feelings of remorse and love towards me and on one occasion was impelled to telephone to me for forgiveness. She did not follow this impulse, however, as she also felt angry with me. The next morning she greeted me with expressions of surprise. She had had an entirely new emotional experience. Throughout the previous afternoon she had been a prey to conflicting feelings: intense impatience with me; anger and fear of anger, mingled with feelings of love for me; and despair at not being able to possess me. She had later gone to a very beautiful concert and had been astonished to find that, although she felt constantly the instinctual battle of love and anger raging in her, she was also able to feel a certain happiness and quiet peace, and a delight in the external circumstances of the evening.

Her next lesson, and the final one of her analysis, she soon learned with great surprise. She found that it is possible and desirable to allow oneself to recognize and to endure these battles of love, longing, need, frustration, anger, and fear, which are a constant accompaniment of life; to keep them, by acknowledging them and not denying them, on a deep but conscious level, thereby freeing the upper levels of consciousness for the minute-by-minute perceptions and reactions of everyday life. After several months of such revaluation, fear of her instinctual conflicts was removed and her constant sense of irremediable damage to herself vanished. The memory of this damage became valued as the evidence of her rich and passionate nature, and as the symbol of her capacity to bear suffering. Thus the more normal expression of her masochistic instinct superseded her lifelong indulgence in the states of depression and self-despising that had previously threatened her existence. She was now able to undertake her life in reality, with a self-esteem based primarily on a new confidence in her instinctive nature and in her endurance.

Ferenczi's belief was that in this active and somewhat violent stage of the analysis, the analyst himself can be less active than heretofore. In the earlier stages he has been obliged constantly to prod the patient out of his defenses and to entice him into greater emotional activity, in order to bring him at the earliest possible moment face to face with the anxiously dreaded situations which have haunted him since their first appearance in his infancy. As his emotional strength increases with exercise and understanding, he at last dares to take this last step, dares to unleash the feelings that have never before been allowed full expression. This he can only do if he is confident that his analyst will protect him against destruction: that of the analyst, of his surroundings, and, in consequence, of himself. For a period of time these impulses are nip and tuck within him. The analyst awaits the outcome. At this moment there needs to be no prodding, no interfering on his part; only an occasional honest expression of his own feelings, when there is danger of a slackening tension. He has initiated the momentum and it will run its course if undisturbed. At this time he need only stand prepared to assist his patient to gain greater strength in self-confidence after he has dared to make the plunge into the sea of his emotions. He waits, as does the mother with her arms outspread to catch the little son as he takes his first running steps. The patient's entire concentration is focused on this critical feat. Its successful outcome opens up a new world to explore.

SIXTH STAGE OF TREATMENT

The patient, relieved at the unexpected outcome of his conflict with the analyst, casts away his distorted sense of values and, learning to measure his growing reality sense by means of the realities of the analytic situation, finds the analytic relationship no longer sufficiently satisfying or necessary to his life adjustment.

The discovery that his neurotic fears were based upon an entirely false premise comes as an overwhelming experience to the patient. That he does not himself disintegrate from the strength of his passions, nor destroy the person who is to him most precious and therefore most frustrating, nor lose his affectionate respect, is astounding to him. He has felt the extreme force of his feelings and cannot belittle it in his own mind. He has also experienced his intense struggle to control it, at first by his neurotic protections against it and finally in his healthier power by expressing it vocally, or even to some extent physically, without bringing about any actual destruction to himself or to anyone else. This more normal control is based on the recognition that he most loves the person at whom his hatred has been directed; that his feelings of resentment and anger are in themselves worthy of respect, and not in any way shameful; and that his deep affection and need for the object of his anger are even stronger and more permanent than his attacks of rage.

The outcome of this final crisis leaves the patient emotionally exhausted, and he turns to the figure of his analyst, again wondering how the latter can have borne with him. He recalls each step of the battle, revaluing it, not through the delusions of his exaggeratedly aggressive feelings but on the realistic basis of justified irritation and of affection. He sees the analyst's tolerance, his patient endurance, and feels blessed in the security that he has found in him. From day to day he more clearly recognizes the many roles that the analyst has been forced by him to play in his phantasy life. He admits into greater consciousness his need to gain his analyst's love and admiring respect. At last, in winning the battle by his own great efforts, he achieves a belief in his endurance and strength. He has attained his integrity. This he recognizes as something of consequence to offer as a reward to his analyst and friend.

These realizations form the kernel of a developing sense of reality which automatically takes the place of the destroyed kernel of his neurosis. The patient now views his personal relationships in their actual light. He knows his own needs and begins to consider not only what their limitations are, but also how they can in reality be satisfied. This again leads him back to his analyst. He longs to keep his new-found security in him, to possess him for himself. But here his budding reality sense and his analyst's admissions make him now aware, slowly and very painfully, that the analyst cannot reciprocate his own feelings. He is already a secure person, with many other interests and concerns. It is true that he has proved without a doubt that he is a devoted and loyal friend, a good and dear parent. The patient is, however, being forced to realize that the analyst has no great emotional need for him. The analyst's wish, as far as he is concerned, is for him to be well and to take over his mature responsibilities. In relinquishing his illness, he must accept separation from his analyst.

Needless to say, this is a difficult stage in the analysis. Here the analyst's tact, subtlety, and honesty are of the greatest moment. To help his patient to evaluate him as he really is, without dissipating his new-found feeling of security in him, demands a meticulous and sympathetic skill. It is probable that the analyst's frank evaluation of his own personality and a willingness to learn from his patient of his own shortcomings, changing them when possible, are among the most essential elements in the development of the patient's growing sense of reality, his tolerance, and his capacity to bear disappointment. Little by little the analyst stands out more and more clearly defined, with his many dissatisfying qualities and his frustrating limitations. This new capacity for critical appraisal deals first with the analyst and spreads later to the whole life of the patient, until he becomes so absorbed in the excitement of realistic living that the analysis no longer holds sufficient interest or value for him.

Example: Exchange of the ghostly illusions of the neurotic past for the actual conditions of the present can be observed in the following example of a patient in the last month of her analysis. She had spent the immediately previous weeks in recognizing her loving devotion to the analyst, her dependence on her, and her wish for an indefinite continuance of the fond maternal care which she had now found for the first time in her life. She had found in me a mother whom she could love, and of whose interest and affection she was sure. Why could she not keep me forever, live with me, rely on me for help in all her problems, spend her days with me as a favorite and beloved daughter? She used many analytic hours in demanding this love, begging for it, insisting upon it. She had finally the courage to ask the reason for my not giving it to her. I explained that I hadn't it to give—that I led a full life as it was, and that there was necessarily but little room in my life for her. To have this actually said to her filled her with despair, as it left her with no hope of obtaining what she so passionately desired and had had the bravery to plead for. Days of grief and frustrated anger alternated.

At this time she planned a week-end in the country near my summer home, and asked me as she was leaving if she could do any errand for me while there. I said that if she really wanted to take the trouble, I should like to have some asparagus picked and brought to me. Her ambivalent reactions were at once apparent. She felt that she was being treated as a servant. This was the kind of demand that her mother would have made on her in return for her affection. The following day she drove over to our farm and looked at the asparagus, deciding to return early the next morning to cut it. It was a beautiful afternoon and she lay on the grass by the house watching the sunset, smoking a cigarette and enjoying the illusion of possessing me. She was there alone with my house, it could not resist her or refuse itself to her. She was in power. She finished her cigarette and, remembering that I had once told her to throw the lighted end onto the short grass where it would safely burn out, she started to do so. A sudden picture of my house in flames flashed across her imagination. She would do what I advised and in so doing she would destroy me. Terror seized her heart and remained there, although she carefully and deliberately extinguished the cigarette end. Each moment of her returning drive she saw herself throwing the lighted end onto the grass and saw the house in flames. All the evening she continued shudderingly to see it. She spent a sleepless, frightened night, impelled several times to dress and start for my farm. Finally at daybreak she drove over, to find the house safe, calm and reassuring in the light of the early dawn.

Again she lay on the grass and smoked a cigarette, pondering over the past twelve hours. As a child she would have obeyed her mother to the letter and have thrown the lighted end onto the grass. If the house had burned down and her mother been killed, it would have been her mother's fault. The terrible compulsion to destroy her mother by meticulously obeying her, and to punish me for my unavoidable withdrawal from her, had been dramatized in the frighteningly realistic phantasy of the afternoon and night. In spite of the compulsion she had not obeyed her mother, had not done what I had advised; instead she had used her own judgment, saving the house and me from destruction, and this despite her sorrowful knowledge that she must soon be denied my maternal care. Here, too, was dramatized her decision at least to keep me in her heart, to cherish me by her own developing maturity. A great sadness and loneliness came over her as she accepted these difficult realities in place of the earlier neurotic illusions. As a little girl she would have forced herself to prove her love for her mother in ways that would have brought angry punishments upon her and have aroused in herself equally angry and destructive wishes. No longer, however, did the passion of anger satisfy her; nor was her passionate love for me of any avail. Only grief seemed left for her.

This week-end experience gave her great confidence in her own intuitive judgment, in her unexpected ability to stand the depths of anxiety and the pain of separation and loss. She no longer feared that she would, in the despair of frustration, destroy what was most precious to her, but found that she could instead preserve her love and maintain her own integrity.

Here we see in a dramatically phantasied form the actual content of the last period of the analytic treatment. Sorrow and the increasing ability to bear sorrow, together with the determination and capacity to find happiness, are the essential characteristics of this final stage. To have won the power to love, to be forced so soon to recognize the tenuousness of the object of one's love, is indeed a grief. To admit one's grief, keeping indestructibly in one's heart the feelings of love, and, in spite of the sorrow of loss, to achieve happiness, is a difficult lesson to learn.

A sense of magic pervades the last step of the analytic process. The dream of victory, of the acquisition of self-sufficiency and integrity, of outgoing love and generous gratitude, of deep need and deprivation, and of grief, is shared with the analyst. As the demands and pleasures of the outside world call more temptingly, and the new strength longs to be exercised, the mature and healthy individual is eager to answer and sees in these calls an opportunity to prove his devotion to his loyal friend and to himself. Every mother knows the experience which the analyst must at this moment undergo. He rejoices and is sorrowful with his patient, but his own happiness lies along the very path which the patient is now intent on following. The final day of the analysis may come unexpectedly, and "Farewell!" is said by two friends of long standing. Analyst and patient now face ahead into the future, relieved that the therapeutic struggle is over and that a well-equipped and maturing human being is re-entering life.

In describing the somewhat arbitrary divisions of the analytic process, and in quoting dialogues, series of dreams and phantasies, behavior during the hour and outside the analysis, from cases illustrative of such periods, I have tried to show a few of the many ways in which a vital relationship between analyst and patient is essential to the success of the analytic therapy. It is this vital relationship which Ferenczi considered the nucleus around which the analyst's technique should revolve. As the cases reported had necessarily to be taken from my own practice, the descriptions and conclusions are, of course, the outcome of my reactions to the individual patients and of my attitude towards the experience of being an analyst. I can only hope that I have succeeded in giving some indication of the broadly human scope of Ferenczi's technique.

Objections to Ferenczi's Technique

I have attempted to summarize the outstanding contributions in the therapeutic technique of Sándor Ferenczi to that of the strictly Freudian school. These have aroused in the psychoanalytic world serious questioning as to possible inherent difficulties. Four such objections stand out most prominently: to the use of the counter-transference as a technical instrument; to the analyst's attitude towards the patient's resistance; to the necessity of reliving early traumatic experience; and to the dramatic tone of the process.

COUNTER-TRANSFERENCE AS TOOL

To use the counter-transference as a technical tool, as one uses the transference, dreams, association of ideas, and the behavior of the patient, seems to many analysts exceedingly dangerous. Much of this anxiety has to do with the analyst's fear of his own impulses, his intuitional weakness, and his lack of self-knowledge. In so far as this is true, it points to the need for further and deeper analysis for the analyst, so that he may strictly and thoroughly know himself and his limitations. But, in addition to this, there is often among analysts a preference for the teacher-pupil relation, a didactic and distant attitude towards the patient, rather than the tender parental attitude. The teacher relation allows the analyst to keep himself apart from his patient, to divulge just enough of his own personality to control the patient's confidence in him, to remain strong and self-assured in the eyes of himself and of his patient, and to give help to the patient as a beneficent gift. The basis of this kind of treatment seems to be anxiety, as evidenced in the analyst's insecurity in himself and in the patient's awe of the analyst. The patient learns because he must, and the hypnotic tie that binds him to the analyst may in the end be far more unbreakable than the tie of tender devotion.

The benefit of the direct and fearless technical use of the counter-transference lies, as I have said before, in the development of a real situation and its use. The analyst, a human being himself, cannot but have emotional reactions to the patient and to their mutual situation. The truth is that in the analytic consulting room there are two people, each living vital lives, each bent on solving one and the same problem, meeting day after day for several years, growing to know each other better with every day. It is impossible to imagine and ludicrous to assert that an emotional relationship on both sides must not inevitably develop in such a setting. It is outside the realm of possibility that an analyst who is sincerely determined to cure his patient does not grow to care for him.

The difference in quality between the analyst's feelings for the patient and the patient's for the analyst lies in the safeguarding fact that the analyst understands his own emotional reactions. This understanding allows him to make right use of his trained and intuitional skill and prevents him from allowing his own personal problems to enter upon the analytic scene. As a patient recently said: "I must trust you not to bring your problems here to me. You should be well enough to settle your own affairs, at least not to burden me with them!" This patient was warning me to watch carefully lest my emotional reactions be unconsciously vented upon him. There is only one source of prevention for this and that is the analyst's thorough understanding and control of himself. This, however, is one of the prime requisites in all analysts. If a technique must guard against the analyst's lack of self-knowledge and self-control, the foremost therapeutic value is lost.

The analyst should be constantly aware of his own personality traits and should constantly take into consideration the fact that they are impinging upon the patient's personality. They should be mutually dealt with, not as the analyst's personal problems, but as facts—which indeed they are. In this way the patient is being exposed over and over again to actualities of his own real situation and derives permanent benefit from the exposure. To seize the most appropriate moment for this experience is an important attribute of the analyst's skill. The content of his reactions does not compare in significance with the time, and with the honest and tactful manner, of their expression. The sure criterion of such technical "activity" is the question: How can I best assist my patient at this particular moment? The analyst should know when the acknowledgment of his own feelings of affection, of confidence, of admiration, of impatience, of weakness, of discouragement, of temporary dislike, of actual incapacity, and the like, can be of benefit. At the beginning of the treatment such an admission often serves to clarify in the patient's mind his own protective mechanisms and focuses his attention on his own habits of thought and behavior. At the critical moments of the analysis the analyst's reactions often raise the tension to the important breaking point and at the same time give the patient courage to face this greatly feared test. During the last period of the analysis such acknowledgments by the analyst help greatly to develop the patient's sense of reality and in the end prove to him that neither the analysis nor the analyst can offer him exclusive satisfaction now that he is well.

In the more usual and didactic form of treatment, the patient is constantly dealing with an unknown quantity as far as the counter-transference is concerned and is at the mercy of the analyst's authority and artificial strength of position. Although such treatment may cure the neurosis, Ferenczi thought it could not lead to a sufficiently thorough and permanent establishment of the patient's personality.

RESISTANCE

The mechanism of resistance is in the minds of most analysts a stumbling block in the path of the cure. It is to be feared and to be dissipated as quickly as possible. This point of view seems to be largely responsible for the generally practiced "passive" technique. As long as the analyst remains as the quiet screen upon which to project the moving picture of the patient's past and present life, the patient's resistances need be dealt with only impersonally and objectively, and therefore with greater ease and less fearsomely, usually by means of interpretation. If the analyst, on the other hand, takes an active part in the analytic process, he comes vividly to life, and the resistances become more powerful and stubborn and tend to be directed at him. Confidence in him, however, is simultaneously increased by his very aliveness and allows the patient to bring the highly charged situation into the open. He feels himself in actual conflict with his analyst, duplicating the difficult or traumatic occurrences of his childhood. That his analyst reacts in his own individual manner and differently from the personalities in the patient's earlier life is a fact that gradually dawns upon his consciousness and finally sweeps away the resistances.

Ferenczi welcomed resistance as an essential part of the patient's emotional make-up. It is in resistance that emotional tension is at its height and that the expression of sheer feeling is given vent to in its most unadulterated form. The result of allowing the tension to increase gradually throughout the analysis, until it becomes unbearable and breaks down the protective barriers, contributes not only to the patient's eventual relief but to the analyst's immediate, and to the patient's ultimate, understanding of the manner in which these highly important parts of his personality have always functioned. It is only in maintaining resistance and increasing it to the breaking point that the patient tends to lose temporarily his sense of reality and can actually become the infuriated, or the impenetrably stubborn, or the desperately forlorn child that he once was. To alleviate the tension by interpreting the resistance, as many analysts do at the end of the analytic hour, deprives the patient of his courageous and needful attempt to relive the moment of his life which he most greatly dreads, and, in so doing, deprives him of his growing potency. This is an easier and less frightening course for the analyst than to maintain the resistances. To watch and encourage the growth of emotional tension is a difficult and anxious task. In this way, however, a lesson is learned by the patient through actual experience which no amount of teaching and explanation can ever accomplish. Such an experience of reliving is for the patient an incontrovertible proof. Both patient and analyst have been preparing for this moment for many months. It does not come suddenly or unexpectedly. But until it is undergone and has become an actual part of the patient's life, this lesson cannot have a sufficiently solid and lasting quality.

RELIVING THE EARLY TRAUMA

The therapeutic necessity for the actual reliving in the analytic situation of early traumatic experience is frequently questioned. Could not the same results be obtained, it has been asked, and the analytic process shortened, by assisting the patient to the emotional experience of gaining insight only? Does not the excitement of at last fully comprehending his method of functioning, without the deeper experience of reliving, make a sufficiently intense and immediate impression upon the patient for him to be able thereafter to call this lesson to his aid at critical junctures and thereby cancel any need to repeat his former neurotic way of life?

Such a situation arose in the case of a young man who, during the first year of analysis, became increasingly convinced that his mother's sudden death, when he was five years old, was responsible for his neurosis. During a certain analytic hour, under great emotional stress, he again reconstructed the death scene. In his loneliness and longing for her during her illness, he had pushed open the door of her bedroom and had immediately been reproved by her in a sad and very tired voice. At this unexpected rebuff the world had fallen from under his feet, and when he was told the next morning of her death it was no surprise. From that time on he, too, had not dared to act as a person alive.

This recovered memory had ended the analytic hour and I had joined my family at tea in the living room. Suddenly the door was pushed open and the haggard face of my patient reappeared. "I must talk to you again!" he said. I returned to my study with him, to be told that at last he understood the crux of the whole death scene. As he was leaving my house he had suddenly realized that when, as a little boy, he had opened the door of his mother's room, he had not known that she was ill, he had not understood her absence from him, and he had in desperation played a kind of mischievous joke on her, pushing the door open and calling "Boo!" at her. She had formerly always responded to this loving play, even when cross or impatient. In delight and loving anticipation, and sure of success, he had thrust open her door, only to be reproved and rejected by her dying voice.

My patient was now overwhelmed by this sudden insight. He was certain that he himself was responsible for his mother's death and that on this childhood experience was based his entire neurotic character of deadness, anxiety, inability to love, refusal to find happiness. He now saw himself in the past as merely marking time, awaiting his own death. That after the analytic hour he had actually and unconsciously dramatized the death scene also made a deep impression on him. His interruption of me, of my privacy, and his demand to see me immediately were the result of his unconscious need to discover whether I, too, would reprove and reject him. That I did not do so, but instead welcomed him and helped him to gain greater insight, initiated the cancellation of the destructive influence of this early trauma. The next morning he felt, in his own words, "as if the spring freshets had begun," "as if the flood gates had been opened." In this instance we have an example of the benefit derived from sudden and exciting insight into the original cause of an entire life of depression and incapacity. He was overwhelmed, not only by this unexpected vision of the most terrible moment in his childhood but also by the extraordinary fact of his actually, and quite unconsciously, reliving that circumstance symbolically in the analysis.

It may be possible that in general such an emotional experience of gaining insight satisfies the therapeutic requirements of most analysts. Ferenczi firmly believed, however, that the neurosis could not be permanently eradicated unless the patient not only recaptures the memory of the early trauma but eventually brings into the analytic framework a dramatic situation between the analyst and himself which perfectly duplicates the original experience. This duplication must be a situation which does not *imitate* the original scene, as did in this case the patient's interruption of me after the analytic hour. It must instead be the introduction into the analytic relationship of an actual set of circumstances which have to do only with the analyst and himself, but which have, however, the identical emotional tension and emotional setup that originally existed. As I have shown in my description of the fifth stage of treatment, the unconscious, if given the opportunity and a sure confidence in the analyst, finally dares to bring such a crisis into existence.

One can foresee that the young man just described will in the future also attempt, in some set of circumstances that concerns me deeply, to intrude upon me personally. This intrusion will undoubtedly be aimed at my emotional life, at a weak and vulnerable part of my personality. He will not make this attempt until he has resurrected in himself his original vivacious, lovable, and loving nature and until he has tested my endurance in many slight and somewhat similar circumstances. The Achilles' heel which he will have acutely discovered in my character should be well known to me and must not be wounded in a surprise attack. Therefore, the chances are good that in this final attempt he will not succeed in forcing me to reject him but instead will himself reject the disastrous effect which his mother's death had upon him as a child of five. This crisis will be a safe reliving of the harmful occurrence of the past in an actual and important situation of the present. No "emotional experience of insight" alone can so certainly prove to him the destructive influence of his early trauma or so permanently destroy his tendency to submit to such an influence.

THE USE OF DRAMA

The same basis for questioning the use of the counter-transference exists in questioning the wisdom and efficacy of allowing the natural drama inherent in all personal relationships to be the dominant theme of the analytic process. We are asked: "Is not the dramatic element a dangerous threat to the success of the technique?" "May it not get out of hand, or seem to the patient like a playful game or artificial trick?" Attention should here be called to the fact that the patient should not sense the drama of the analysis to the extent that the analyst does, if at all. He should only be conscious of his capacity for feeling more and more strongly as the analysis proceeds. The analyst, on the other hand, with a firm grip on the reality of the situation, is merely responding to the patient's increasing emotional strength. His own feelings, in contrast to the patient's, remain in comparison quantitatively the same throughout the analysis. It is mainly for this reason that the process grows more and more dramatic in tone—for this reason, and because the patient's emotional tension is constantly approaching the critical breaking point.

Certainly this dynamic type of analysis is more dangerous in unskilled, unwise, and unsure hands than is a more intellectual and didactic type. Analysts, like their patients, tend to seek refuge in mental concepts and to function therapeutically on a mental level. They do this as a protection, for they fear to participate in an emotional drama. Undoubtedly they thereby obtain therapeutic results. But could they not approach more closely to the kernel of the illness if they used the emotional language of the unconscious, if they attempted to work on its own dramatic level? Would they not be more likely to eradicate the neurosis, and then to assist in the maturing of the individual, if they dealt with him on an instinctive and feeling basis?

Again we must look at the life of the child, where every waking moment is intensely significant and is a stream of highly charged emotions. The more completely we are to undo the harm of those early years, the more closely must we approximate to their conditions. It must here be repeated that to take an appropriate and beneficial part in the analytic drama, the analyst needs a sure knowledge of himself, a capacity to use himself as a technical instrument, and the possession of a carefully trained talent. Without these assets, it is certainly wiser to treat the patient from an intellectual point of view.

Ferenczi's Contributions to the Freudian Technique

Ferenczi's therapeutic technique is not in any way a departure from the basic principles of Freud's psychoanalytic discoveries. It is firmly based on the theories of the unconscious, of repression, of identification, of infantile sexuality, of the repetition compulsion; and on those of the pleasure-unpleasure principle, and on the division of personality into id, ego, and superego. Association of ideas, interpretation of the symbolic language of the unconscious and of dreams, the transference, the counter-transference, resistance—all are essential technical instruments in Ferenczi's treatment. An analysis by him was similar to a Freudian analysis, except in its vital and dramatic tone and in the importance of active and cherishing participation by the analyst. For, as Ferenczi had discovered, " 'Healing' is the reassuring effect of encouragement and of tenderness."[3]

The psychoanalytic process was to Ferenczi a deeply emotional human experience, a living experience as intense and dynamic as Freud showed the life of early childhood to be, with its great conflict between instinctual and repressive forces. The treatment should not be a mere part of a patient's life, isolated and comparatively unrelated, as is the usual medical treatment by a physician or the usual educational course of lessons by a teacher. It should comprise the whole of a patient's life for the time being, as a child's life with his family forms the framework for every activity, thought, and feeling, whether inside or outside the home. The simpler, more direct, more feeling and more human the process is, the more it duplicates the much needed natural warmth of the child's home experience. The more complicated, intellectual, and impersonal it is, the more it represents the forces against which the child has had to contend. For the analysis to be of real and lasting avail, the patient's heart must be deeply touched. It is not sufficient to re-educate him.

In extent, Ferenczi's analytic treatment had no set limits. To help the patient gradually to gain the strength to re-experience the original trauma or traumatic series of experiences was always his hope. Or, if it was a case of long exposure to a cruel environment, as is so frequently true, to re-experience this exposure over and over again, and with increasing tension, seemed essential to a permanent cure. Such a far-reaching operation usually means a very long analytic treatment. This Ferenczi constantly endeavored to ameliorate. How to journey as far but in less time was

[3] Quoted in the "Ferenczi Number," *International Journal of Psycho-Analysis*, Vol. XXX, Part 4, 1949.

an ever-present problem to him. The answer to this problem, he thought, lay in the role of the analyst. His chief part, in addition to the application of his skill in understanding and in interpretation, should consist in raising the tension between himself and the patient in proportion to the patient's endurance. This, as we have seen, means taking an active part in a highly emotional relationship. The purpose of this is to strengthen the patient, but much more importantly to bring finally and very carefully to a head the threatening dramatic crisis.

In this crisis the seed of the neurosis is detached and brought forth. In truth, this is a rebirth. The essential characteristics of parenthood, therefore, were to Ferenczi the essential characteristics of the analyst. Clear understanding of oneself, depth of feeling and human kindness, humility, high imagination, great patience and endurance, fearlessness, a capability to learn and an ability to teach by example rather than by precept—these are as necessary elements in the analyst's capacity as is his carefully acquired skill. Sándor Ferenczi little knew, as he so painstakingly and with much opposition labored at his psychoanalytical research, that these characteristics summarized to a high degree his own rich personality.

Chapter 3

LOVE AND ANGER: THE TWO ACTIVATING FORCES IN PSYCHOANALYTIC THERAPY

To a large extent the concern with therapeutic theories and methods is caused by an uncertainty as to the nature of "cure." Does "cure" mean ridding the patient of his most troublesome neurotic symptoms, or does it also include his emotional re-education? Does it mean assisting the patient to recover sufficient mental and emotional balance so that he may return to his "reality situation" and remain there without further breakdown? Or does it also include the replacement of his neurotic personality with a character which stems from his specific constitution and becomes the outgrowth of his inner integrity, heretofore buried and suffocated beneath the neurotic edifice? Or, finally, does psychoanalytic therapy have as its goal a physically, mentally, and emotionally integrated person?

Whichever may be the chosen definition of the ultimate aim, it affects the technique of each school of psychoanalytic therapy and of the individual therapist. Hence great differences in methods and rules are found. Is it not possible, in spite of these differentiations, to formulate certain principles which underlie all types of technique and form the dynamic substructure upon which psychoanalytic therapy rests?

Freud was the first clearly to define and draft a chart of the development of human personality. He specified the reefs upon which it can be wrecked and gave warning of the various types of disaster to be expected. Upon the basis of this chart of discovery he may be said to have initiated a science of human navigation. Not only did he teach the psychological laws of human behavior, but also the methods of guarding against accidents to the personality and of repairing the damage once the accident has occurred. He demonstrated that underlying the physical and mental systems there is a vast emotional realm, hitherto unexplored. Here the currents of love and hate, and the related emotions, are blocked or unleashed in the stress and strain of life.

The knowledge of this foundation has increased with the years. The various emotions and their sources can now be more specifically labeled and recognized. It is known at what points in character development they may be expected to appear—and at what points the capacity for their expression may be almost completely destroyed. There is, in other words, a growing knowledge of these forces, from a descriptive point of view. But has scientific use of this knowledge, or of the forces as instruments in the development of character and in the repair of wrecked personalities, yet been learned?

The manner in which psychoanalytic treatment helps to renovate such wrecks is well known. Many techniques have come into existence, each of which boasts some success, but the reason for the success of these methods and what their activating principles may be has been little studied. It is my wish to offer here some suggestions as to the dynamic basis of the psychoanalytic process.

The person hoping to benefit from this treatment is suffering in his neurosis from an inability, for one reason or another, to adjust to the various demands of living among his fellow men. He is surrounded by all types of personality, each of whom has also his own particular character assets and liabilities. It seems reasonable to reduce all the external accompaniments of character, such as material success or failure, good or bad health, desirable opportunities, and the cultural mores of particular societies, to the basic determinant, one's fellow man. From man's exposure to his companions in living comes, in the last analysis, the manner of creating his own environment. The child is born possessed of the passionate desire to grow, to fulfill his capacities in every direction. Although his inherited constitution may modify the various expressions of this desire, it is essentially of untold strength and endurance and forces its way around all obstacles. But it must follow the grooves which the impress of living necessarily offers. This pressure is at bottom caused by the close contact of other personalities. Hence, in studying the dynamic structure of neurotic characters, the premise may be posited that all character development is the result of reaction to other human beings.

The possession of emotions is common to all men. These lie beneath all action and thought, and even perhaps beneath physiological weaknesses and strengths. They are like currents in the ocean depths from which each surface ripple originates. This ocean depth in each person touches through the upper currents that of every other proximate person. Results to both differ with each case. So, although men have the passionate growth impulse in common, no two men can ever be alike; each is the result of the surging of this passion around the dams and through the grooves into which the meeting with other human beings thrusts it. This is the basis of human struggle.

It may be said that the urge to live and grow represents the joy and exhilaration of life, the love and creative impulses; the dams and groove banks represent the frustrations, the anger and despair, the destructive impulses. Certainly, in a newborn creature, the determination to obtain what is needed for living is the envy and admiration of all who behold. Almost immediately, and influenced generally by the presence of others, this determination results in complete blissfulness or rage. Slowly these complete emotions become broken down and modified to fit the varying circumstances of the developing child. It may, therefore, be said that love and anger are the intrinsic fundamental emotions, and that it is on the basis of the conflict between these two forces and between their appropriate modifications that human beings form their characters.

It is now easily seen why comparatively happy and successful or creative persons develop from the persistent victory of love over anger. This seems a truism. There is less willingness, however, to consider that the unhappiness, maladjustment, and failure of human beings arise from the conquest of their loving nature by the fierceness of hatred.

If this latter be true, one may see that in all neuroses, perhaps in all illness, one is confronted by the results of a raging but unconscious struggle between these two emotions and in a partial success of the destructive forces. This being so, the therapeutic treatment necessarily becomes a continuance of this struggle, but with the clear objective of a change in outcome.

Love must conquer hatred if the patient is to live a happy creative life. And this means living to his full capacity, undeterred by the blocking effects of destructive anger, envy, and jealousy. The removal of these obstructing evils in a patient's character and the growth of his capacity to exercise and mature his inherent constructive nature can only be finally achieved by the patient, but this achievement must be in relation to another human being. This human being should have already learned a way of nullifying the evil effects of anger in himself and be able to avail himself of his skill and training through the unobstructed use of his creative impulses. Hence, the mutual relationship of patient and physician is not only a problem in the dynamics of personality, it is also an ethical and moral problem.

The very act of seeking help in the many difficulties that beset a neurotic person is an admission that he has failed in his personal relations.

Neurotic illness is accompanied by unhappiness and a sense of impotence and failure, whether it is manifested in hysterical symptoms, in obsessions and compulsions, in behavior problems, or in character defects. Beneath all such symptoms lie anger and hatred, with accompanying anxiety. It is the analyst's prime concern to seek for the original sources of these deterrents, uproot them, and give actual space to his patient's capacity to love. Herewith the creative impulses flood in, in proportion to the space available. This phenomenon, a living proof that "nature abhors a vacuum," is in effect a constant miracle.

Phases in the Shift of Emotional Content, Quality, and Emphasis during Psychoanalytic Treatment

The analytic process may be described, from the point of view of this thesis, as consisting in a constant change in emotional content, quality, and emphasis, due primarily to the varying elements in the relationship of patient to analyst. In this change three phases become distinct: (1) in making the acquaintance of the figure and personality of the analyst, the patient gradually rids himself of his defenses, begins to sense strongly his repressed hostility and to become dimly aware of his tender feelings; (2) in taking account of, and struggling with, this personality, which has for the moment become the center of his life, the patient dares to give vent to his impulses of hatred; and (3) in resolving this struggle, the patient, increasingly freed from anxiety, gains the courage to release his loving and creative impulses as well as to make constructive use of his anger. As a result, a successful and productive relationship is established with the analyst, which will constitute a lasting pattern in personal relations.

The designation of three periods of treatment in the delineation of the emotional change and development of the neurotic patient in no way contradicts the diagrammatic division into six stages of the total over-all view of the psychoanalytic process, as outlined in the previous chapter. There we examined in detail the *mechanisms* by means of which the patient successfully rids himself of his neurosis. Here we are examining another aspect of the patient's development—the *growth in emotional maturity* from that of unconscious hostility to that of the conscious and ripening capacity to love.

FIRST PERIOD OF TREATMENT

The patient's protective neurotic edifice crumbles, and there is an accompanying indirect expression of hostility and a tentative awareness of the tender impulses.

Early months of analytic treatment are dedicated to a careful and tactful uncovering of the basic emotional conflict. That so much time has passed before the destructive impulses have finally conquered and reduced the patient to illness betokens the degree of entrenchment behind which they are protected. As this battle has been won gradually, so must the motion of cure as gradually put the hitherto victorious forces into reverse. The analyst's strong ally is always the patient's thwarted impulse for creative growth; but this impulse is distrustful, easily frightened, and vulnerable. It has already lost too many battles to expose itself readily to further tests.

These tests, however, are now necessary to the building up of the patient's confidence in the analyst and in himself; their success lies in the fact that, due to the analyst's understanding and endurance, the patient, to his surprise, suffers no untoward consequences. They begin with the first professional interview. Some element in the analyst's character and skill offers, all unconsciously to the sufferer, a dim hope that the tables may at last be turned. This appears to him actually to be occurring as the analysis is begun and continues. The analyst seems to the patient to change from a kind, skillful doctor in a professional office to a kind, interested friend in an easy, comfortable setting, more a companion and less a figure in authority. This change is the result on the patient's part of a semiconscious and diffident, but constant, trying out of the analyst by means of slight and tentative expressions of his reactions, especially those of hostile criticism. These are, when necessary, skillfully elicited by the analyst and are directed toward figures in the patient's past or present environment, and, finally, toward the analyst himself. That this hostility is not irretrievably entrenched is seen in its very reluctance to be dislodged and in the anxiety that accompanies each step of dislodgement. It has, in the neurosis, become the patient's chief power and tends stubbornly to be preserved against all the seeming wiles of the analyst. Yet the patient gradually becomes aware that it forms the main obstruction to his health and happiness. With this awareness comes the fear that he will fail in removing this obstruction; despair and increased anxiety result.

Experience has heretofore seemed to prove to him that the loving and tender impulses are easily wounded and will inevitably be trampled upon and extinguished. Yet now there has at last appeared upon the scene a fellow human being who gives promise of being trustworthy, who may value these frail impulses for themselves. The temptation and attempt to trust the analyst come to the patient after a long period of guarding himself by the various ways of expression and behavior which he had found to be acceptable to, or at least protective in, his former environment. With this new endeavor comes the acceptance of a slow willingness in himself to let drop these defenses and give vent to expressions of sincere feeling, which, in the nature of the emotional experiences of his past, tends to take shape as antagonism. Not having discomfited his analyst by such expressions, the patient finds a continued courage to voice a slightly more direct hostility. With this there comes inevitably a further flood of anxiety.

Can it be possible that the familiar experience of punishment and loss will not reoccur, at the hands this time of his much-needed analyst? May not this new friend suddenly prove ready to threaten and punish when anger cries aloud? That this feared result does not occur somewhat allays the patient's worry and confusion, and there is seen for the first time the timid entrance upon the stage of tender impulses in his emotional relief, his expressions of appreciation, and his wonder at the seeming miracle.

Example: This train of circumstances in the early period of analysis may be exemplified in the case of a young woman who came to me because of constant failure in her personal relations.

She was the only child of parents old enough to be her grandparents. The father was a sufferer from frequent and severe depressions and used his neurosis as a powerful weapon to control the inmates of his household. The mother lived in terror of her husband's moods and trained her daughter to guard her every move and expression so that the father's equanimity should be undisturbed. This was the more difficult as he seized upon every occasion to bemoan his martyrdom. The mother's discipline of her daughter was made more severe by her feeling of social inferiority and her attempts to conform to social custom.

In this environment the child could develop no character of

her own. Every impulse was stillborn, no judgment could mature. Her entire energy was absorbed in closely imitating her mother's way of life. There grew in her a sense of uselessness, of being of no value in her own right, of having no existence of her own. Her only compensation was an occasional opportunity to arouse her parents' pride in her achievements.

They were ambitious for her. This allowed her some free expression, and it is significant that after college she seized upon a theatrical career as a profession. In this she repeated the perpetual quality of pretense in her childhood and by it she was now enabled blamelessly to leave her life of servitude at home. In addition to this, she found on the stage an opportunity to express the emotions which had been pent up throughout her whole life. But the fact that she was acting a part and not truly expressing her own feelings prevented their complete release. These repressed emotions soon found outlet in increasingly disastrous external circumstances, to her unhappiness and despair, and drove her to seek aid from psychoanalytic treatment.

Her appearance, when she came to me, was that of an attractive, well-mannered, well-dressed young woman; subdued and tense. She agreed to all the conditions of treatment with eagerness and a slight condescension, but from the moment she first lay down on the analytic couch she began persistently to wring her hands, only interrupting this gesture by clasping her neck as if she were being strangled. The material of her contemporary difficult relations was told with anger and a sense of martyrdom and in a highly dramatic manner.

To this latter I drew her attention. As was to be expected, she conformed immediately and attempted to control the melodramatic expression. The wringing of her hands, however, became so incessant that I then drew her attention to it, suggesting that it might symbolize despair and hopelessness. Upon this she poured forth the story of her childhood. Gradually she saw the similarities in the recent unhappy events with those of her family circumstances, and could realize the intense anger toward her parents. This was especially directed toward her father, now a man of eighty years.

Her mother's death, ten years previously, had left her exposed to his idiosyncrasies with no guide or protectress. She gradually realized that she had no existence in his eyes except as she affected his life; that he had no love for her herself nor wish for her happiness. She also became gradually aware of her fury at his constant frustration of her every wish, and at the theft and misuse of her true nature by both parents.

With this anger came a slight tendency to stand up to her father for her own rights. As the months of analysis went by, this increased until she found herself wishing and able to confront him with a demand that their house be mortgaged in order to pay her bill for my services. The carrying out of the wish gave evidence of a semiconscious but increasing valuation of my care of her as opposed to her anger at him for his neglect.

In the meantime, she had found work that interested her, and was studying to increase her skill. She was surprised at the pleasure and relief in the manual labor of a laboratory when compared with her life on the stage. She succeeded in making congenial acquaintances and in becoming of value to her employer.

Through these first six months I had noticed that she excluded me entirely from her calculations. I seemed barely to exist for her. She greeted me politely and spoke of the weather each day on arrival; and she left in the same manner. One time when I became ill she expressed her concern, but did not come to see me at the hospital or write to me when I went South for a month, although I had expressed hope of hearing from her. I had not brought myself to her attention during the previous months, except for occasionally comparing some fact of her situation in the analysis with facts of her past. This omission on my part was due to her intense concentration on the figures of her parents whom she now saw, as it were, face to face, realistically appraising them for the first time.

With the growth of her ability to face her father, culminating in her actual stand against him, there came a pause in the analytic tension, and I took the opportunity to direct her notice to me. The first months had been spent in the expression of great anger, not only at her parents in the past and her father in the present, but at almost everyone with whom she had ever come in contact. It now remained to be seen what she would make of me. As I drew myself to her attention there arose in her a new flood of anxiety accompanied by a renewed wringing of her hands and by the strangling gesture. Her resistance expressed itself in her description of me as cold, stony, plutocratic, and aristocratic. She took refuge in my professional status, to which she attributed my kindness, my gentle voice, my wish to have her write me when ill, my sympathetic understanding, and the help which I had given her. When I asked her if these qualities could not also belong to me as a human being, apart from my profession, she became anxious and confused, confessing that she would be lost if someone were kind and loving to her because of real affection.

"It would frighten me to feel like a human being myself, and I wouldn't know what to do if you were one."

Her lifelong reactions had hitherto been directed toward protecting herself from the threatening people who surrounded her. Her rage at this frustration of her natural loving impulse had been accompanied by great anxiety. Therefore, the tendency at this time in her analysis was to continue anxiously to dodge her issue with me. She became aware of this and diligently tried to focus her attention on me. The struggle was so severe that she succumbed to an acute infection and was put to bed. The analytic hours were continued at her bedside, and she confessed that, when a child, sickness had been her only refuge. She could not then be blamed or disciplined, and she gained the semblance of care and cherishing. This was now being repeated in the kindness of her new acquaintances and in my coming to see her each day.

"If I thought you came because you really cared for me, I would fling myself into your arms!" she exclaimed one day to her great surprise. But when I asked her what she thought might happen if she did, her imagination could go no further. Such a situation seemed to her entirely incredible, impossible to imagine.

Here is seen a victim of thirty years' exposure to severe and unjust training at her mother's hands, to the constantly threatening melancholia and martyrdom of her father, and to their joint annihilation of her mental and emotional wholeness. Her only contact with the loving emotions of her parents was in their ambitious pride in her. There was no respect for her as an independent entity. As a result, the outgoing impulses of affection within her at her birth were deeply buried. Anger and hatred consumed her. These were in turn repressed by the thorough discipline of her frightened and conforming mother. By identification with this mother, she maintained her existence, paying the price through constant difficulties with everybody she came in contact with. In bringing her conforming and anxious mannerisms to consciousness, the analysis had succeeded also in bringing to the surface her hostility. The expression of that in turn had released some small and tentative degree of frightening tender feelings. In this way the battle between anger and love was reoccurring.

SECOND PERIOD OF TREATMENT

The patient expresses his hostility toward the analyst directly, and there occurs a slight release of loving tendencies.

In the history of the young woman previously described is seen an example of the introductory section of psychoanalytic therapy. In this instance, the superficially suppressed emotion of hatred had been slightly released and the deeply repressed affectionate impulses had, with diffidence, shown some signs of life. The central portion of the analytic experience consists essentially in the patient's not only taking stock of the analyst's character as it appears in its varied repetitive guises, but in dealing in actuality with these guises. His manner of so doing is the result of the youthful lessons learned—with trial and tribulation—in reaction to the characteristics of members of his family and of his intimate surroundings. The fact that the analyst does not possess the anticipated characteristics, but reacts with patience and understanding, gradually invalidates the need of the patient to protect himself. It also enables him to recognize that these protections were originally acquired as a means of controlling the expression of his spontaneous feelings of love and anger and despair.

As the need to defend himself against the analyst weakens, the hostile emotions come more freely to the surface. While anxiety is struggling to restrain their expression, the analyst encourages their freedom by his receptivity, his skill in interpretation, and the voicing of his own actual attitudes and character. This task of the analyst plays an important part in loosening the hold which the patient has upon the coming to life of his passionate nature.

The emotion of love can be effectively relegated to oblivion or to a state of impassivity by the presence of hatred; and it is quite impossible for it to exist in action as long as hostility overrides it. All tender or cooperative expressions superimposed on a state of anger can only represent the anxious desire to palliate circumstances, to offer the pretense of not being angry. It is, therefore, essential in the continuance of the analytic treatment to pierce through these unconscious pretenses to the very anger itself, which is holding imprisoned the creative impulses. As anger, now at last in safety to the patient, seeps through its protections, affection also comes nearer the surface, occupying the space left empty by the expressed hostility. This dynamic train of circumstances can be inevitably counted upon. Hence the prime object in psychoanalytic treatment consists in freeing the hostile emotions, allowing entrance to the love impulses, and finally assisting these latter to mature and become firmly established.

Example: As an example of the central part of the analytic process I shall describe the struggle of a young man who had experienced, at the age of two and a half, the partial annihilation of his inner self. The memory of this experience was deeply ingrained but its effect was lost to consciousness.

The youngest of a large family, he had as an infant been secure in the love of both parents. Unexpectedly this unquestioned trust was swept aside in the following manner. From the nursery he heard the laughter and gaiety of a masquerade party downstairs. He caught glimpses from the landing of the strange costumes, the long cloaks, large hats and masks. His mother unexpectedly appeared by his side and, taking off his clothes and giving him a tiny bow and arrow, told him to run downstairs naked to "be Cupid for the ladies and gentlemen." He was overcome with fear and horror and struggled to resist, only to be told that if he loved her he must do as she wished.

It seems that he suddenly sensed her *use* of him, her sacrifice of him for her own pleasure. Her previous devotion became falsified for him and the world was swept from under him. Nothing now mattered except to get the shameful experience over as soon as possible. In despair and disillusion he was dragged downstairs to be met by an outburst of laughter.

Of his return to the nursery he has no memory. From that moment apparently he lost his existence as an integrated whole. His life was now given over to the cancellation and forgetfulness of the earlier falsified experience of the joy of loving and of being loved, to the realization of the dangers of his angry rebellion, and to the creation of a complicated system of defense against both loving and hating. This system took, over a period of many years, the form of emotional deadness and mental incapacity to understand significances. He can be described as merely going through the motions of being alive. No emotional or mental alertness could be discerned despite an exceptionally high intelligence quotient and a gifted temperament.

The first period of his analysis entailed a long struggle on my part to assist this patient to come to life. Months were spent watching him go through the automatic motions of living. No thought or act was spontaneous; each was but a reaction to stimuli, a reaction based on completely inaccurate observation and on a misunderstanding of such stimuli. A smile or invitation, for example, meant to him that he was loved; a serious discussion meant that he was disliked, despised. Therefore he must act to entice pleasant expressions from those around him and must never allow himself to fail in this enterprise. He must have good manners, act as everyone wished and expected; he must train his ability and mind to meet the apparent approval of those around him; and he must never under any circumstances invite laughter or disapproval.

What was even more disastrous to his emotional health, he

must never allow himself to sense or to explore the possibilities as to whether he was in actuality loved or not loved. He put his entire faith in his misinterpretation of superficial signs. Under these false assumptions there lay a thick semiconscious layer of distrust of others, and of belief that no one liked him at all because he was, or so he believed, a "louse." His emotional blindness was such that he was almost entirely unaware of his own unhappiness. Although he came to me for help, he thought he was happy; and this despite the fact that his way of life proved him to be a lonely, frightened, and despairing boy.

In direct contrast to his dull automatism and to his mistaken assumptions, the report of his Rorschach test described his brilliance and native gifts as follows:

"The outstanding endowments of this personality, as revealed in the Rorschach experiment, are a very superior intellect, sensitive powers of observation, rich imagination, and ample creativity. . . . Very superior intelligence is indicated beyond any question; S. must stand in the highest one per cent of the population. . . . Intellectual energy is high . . . S.'s mind is unusually well balanced, his splendid powers of observation keeping him always in excellent touch with reality and practicality. . . . Among his talents the most prominent place is perhaps held by sensitive observation. He seems to have the interests and gifts of a naturalist. . . . One can imagine that like Audubon he might paint, or like Thoreau describe, animals in a way that would be esteemed for both artistic beauty and scientific precision. On the other hand . . . he may be capable of a wider range of creativity. . . . Responses are particularly rich in detail, careful as to form, and original, indicating strong imagination and creative gifts which are capable of mobilizing in their service his observational and critical capacities."

The test draws further attention, however, to ". . . a decided gap between capacity and actual achievement. . . . Adaptation to the surrounding world, especially emotional rapport with people, appears to be unsatisfactory to a degree which has to be considered neurotic."

In appearance and execution he was, as has been said, dull and scarcely alive, an uncut jewel easily mistaken for a piece of thick glass. It could be foreseen that without help in piercing through this glazed surface his entire life would be wasted. Many months were passed in gently calling his attention to the inaccuracy of his interpretation and understanding. At first, he would seem to agree with me and attempt to conform in action with my ideas. He then discovered this insincerity in himself and began to sense the slow disruption of the whole system of false observation and reaction which he had manufactured.

Upon this his anxiety increased, necessitating in him an almost conscious determination to maintain his former false organization. This he could not succeed in recapturing, and with its failure there came to the surface a ray of light. For a moment he caught, with excited pleasure, a glimpse within himself of "the indestructible me." But any expression on my part that could, however incorrectly, be interpreted by him as reproof or disapproval again extinguished his hope and renewed his despair. He would then bring stubborn arguments to bear, attempting to prove his happiness and his capabilities.

When I remarked that these were not apparent, he gave up the struggle of pretense and at last admitted that he did not know what it meant to wish for anything from life or to work for the fulfillment of any such wish, to trust or to be trusted, to love or to be loved. That disaster would result from this despairing admission, and would also accompany the birth of any wishful spark, seemed to him inevitable.

Once more the struggle of frightened despair ended in acute hostility.

With each renewal of this conflict his passionate impulses had come more and more to life. He looked and acted more like a living person, less like an automaton. This was evidenced in a change of occupation, an enjoyment of the new work, a budding ambition, the furtherance of his wish to learn a foreign language, and the establishment of new friendships.

With each new step, however, he repeatedly fought the battle between his constructive impulses, his awkwardness in pursuing them, his consequent frustration, and the ensuing anxiety and anger. The emergence of hostility, as the final step of each new struggle, broke the vicious circle and occasioned the renewal of his creative strength and desire to live fully in reality.

The future direction of the analysis seemed clear: he would so desire a loving and constructive life that he would become a lovable person, capable of realizing his unusual innate capacities. This success would be attained by the use of my personality in place of that of his mother, as a battleground for the passionate impulses of love and anger which for some twenty-five years had remained stultified, immature, and concealed from his conscious life.

THIRD PERIOD OF TREATMENT

The patient acknowledges his love for the analyst and the value of constructive anger.

By unraveling the various protective strands which conceal not only the neurotic person's hostile impulses but also his more deeply buried and vulnerable tender impulses, the essential conflict of the neurosis is disclosed. As each of these emotions is alternately expressed, the other grows in strength until the situation is finally reached in which each has attained full power. Anxiety is proportionately aroused and is attached to the expression both of anger and love. It is finally overcome by increasing trust in the analyst, by a conscious determination to win the battle for health, and by the very strength of the emotional conflict itself. This new emotional setup now seizes and occupies the entire analytic scene.

The antagonistic and protagonistic emotions and their expression come in such quick succession that at times they seem to be superimposed upon each other, first one and then the other being uppermost. A great change is sensed in this last stage of the analysis by both patient and analyst.

The intensity of emotional quality creates a vibrant vitality in the patient's personality. The foundation on which this final period rests changes also in character from anxious despair to determined and hopeful endeavor. The old patterns of self-protection and self-destruction have given place to insistent effort toward successful cure. The sensing of these changes marks in the analyst's mind the turning point of the analytic process, "the home stretch."

It also marks the most severe conflict of the analysis, most severe because the many tangential ways of escape are no longer of avail and have been discarded. The cards are now on the table and must be played. Sufficient mental health has been recovered to encourage the patient to attempt this last hurdle with determination and the hope of success.

Although several years of analytic treatment may have been needed to bring the deeply repressed angry impulses to full direct expression, the anxiety of the patient accompanying this earlier effort is as nothing in comparison with that experienced in the last and shorter period of treatment: the fear of loving, of expressing this love, and of demanding love in return. This impulse is easily wounded. It has no weapon to use in its own right and can only return in defense to the use of hostility, which in itself is a denial of the very impulse which is making use of it. This complete reversal is paradoxical and throws the person into a state of anxiety and confusion. He knows that he loves and longs to be loved.

In his vulnerability he suddenly finds himself hating the very person whom he loves, and whom he is actually aware that he loves. How to make his way successfully through this dense maze is a problem which consumes every moment of his waking and sleeping life. His dreams are concerned with it, and the activities of his daily life are shot through with the undercurrent of this struggle. In this last stage of analysis there is a greater sense of immediate and conscious conflict than at any other period. Every emotion of the patient is now conscious; there are, pragmatically speaking, no more repressions; the original infantile conflict is now on the surface in an adult form and in an adult environment.

A life and death struggle is in process. Its outcome, however, must be victorious. The loving impulses finally brought to life and expression are in their very nature constructive; whereas the hostile impulses, hitherto based on illusion and now in their last battle, are destructive. The patient knows that final victory of the loving impulses leads to the satisfactions of living. They are in essence self-preservative.

Example: The promise of this final victory is exemplified in the case of a young man suffering from homosexual and alcoholic compulsions and from a deep sense of the worthlessness of life. His youth had held no experience of loving security. Born into a luxurious and spendthrift family, he had known only the care of nurses and tutors.

He had been enchanted but neglected by his mother. He could remember the despair of watching her leave the house in company with men other than his father; and with this desertion, a sudden hatred and wish that she were dead. In his early adolescence came the shame of his parents' divorce, the baffling visits to his highly emotional and hypercritical mother, and the custodianship of his father, full of anger and blame toward the wife. For his father he seems at that time to have felt some tender affection and loyalty. This was soon abused by a brutal sexual attack, which occurred suddenly, and was repeated over a period of four years. The result was an almost insane confusion of mind and feelings. His heart was torn between his former affection for his father, his physical and emotional dependence on him, and a new-found terror of him and shame for himself.

He could turn to no one for help in this crisis. As a result he continued the motions of the necessary acts of living and buried the frightening distraction beneath his consciousness. Photographs of him at this age look like those of a feeble-minded child, nor could he afford to develop his thinking powers or his understanding.

Although circumstances later separated him from his father, his course of self-destruction continued, manifesting itself in unsuccessful attempts to be self-supporting, in unhappy love affairs with older men, and in a generally dissolute life.

It is extraordinary that he retained sufficient instinct for self-preservation to seek aid from psychoanalytic treatment. He could not even pretend to any happiness or success in living, when he came to me. His whole energy was devoted to protecting the secret of the disgraceful treatment by his father. He could therefore be very frank about his contemporary homosexuality and alcoholism.

That he had a deeper and more shameful secret, however, appeared from the many mannerisms that bespoke a high degree of false pride. It was as if he were covered with painful bruises. What might be mistaken for hostile gestures on my part toward him caused sudden and angry withdrawals and immediate threats that he would drive his car at full speed over an embankment or that he would leave the analysis at once and forever. The threats were invariably accompanied by bouts of drinking or a new homosexual attachment.

He had never before understood that these two compelling tendencies were suicidal, despairing, and indirect attempts to put the only life he knew behind him; and that they represented the wish of his adolescent years to leave his father, to die if need be. They also, by self-punishment, canceled his shame and guilt, and effectively put the blame upon his parents, with the wish to punish them severely. The knowledge that all of this was involved in his self-destructive compulsions helped to deprive them of their intense energy and released some appreciative gestures toward me for my understanding and for my lack of blame of him.

It is easy to imagine the ups and downs of the course of this patient's analysis, as he became aware of his anger toward both parents for their neglect and abuse of him.

A long period elapsed before he recognized any wish to determine his own fate or any belief that this was possible. Such wishes finally came to consciousness with the clearing of his mental confusion, which had become increasingly centered around me. The first sign of this change was apparent in a new mode of life. He found work that held good future possibilities, lived alone for the first time, began to lose his fear of women, and made new friends of both sexes. He soon discovered, however, that he was allowing me to play no part in this newly constructed life.

With this recognition came the fear that I, like his father, would destroy all that he was so carefully building up. At the same time he desperately needed my support. He could go just so far alone, and then his need to be sure of my trust and love would overwhelm him.

So the battle of need, frustration, distrust, fear of cruel treatment, and anger constantly repeated itself. Each period of conflict resulted in greater attachment to me, in greater demands on me, and it was clearly apparent that the analysis had worked back to his original difficulties with his loved but neglectful mother. He recognized that, had it not been for his mother's negligence and desertion, the shameful abuse at the hands of his father would never have occurred. Hence he was determined to force me to take care of him by every wile at his command.

That I did not succumb to his "basket of tricks," as he called his indirect tendencies, enraged him, and he accused me of being powerless. To this I readily agreed. This accusation comes inevitably in every analysis and is one of the signs that the turning point of the treatment has been reached, when the patient himself is about to take conscious and direct charge of his cure. This patient had finally learned to understand himself. It now remained for him to give up his attempts to beguile me into protecting him and instead to use his self-knowledge purposefully. I could not force him to do this. If he refused to "be himself," I was powerless.

At this juncture I was planning a short holiday. He seized the opportunity to revenge himself on me for this, and for my impotence, by succumbing again to a self-destructive situation. He did not make use this time of the alcoholic elements of his former disasters, but contrived to submit to an almost exact repetition of his father's abuse. This experience said to me as if in words: "You are like my mother. You won't take care of me. You go away and neglect me. I wish you were dead. You don't love me, so I'll kill myself." The shame that accompanied this misuse of himself overwhelmed him. He fell ill, suffering from an attack of hives. His mental and emotional confusion increased. But accompanying it was an ultimate determination to take care of himself and an awareness that to do so he must "be himself"—that he could not afford to be otherwise, and that he no longer needed my maternal care, but instead preferred my affectionate trust and belief in him. The very strength of his rage against me, as seen in his last compulsive action, gave him a sense of the strength of his personality, which he now determined to use constructively. The battle to preserve and to make use of his loving and creative powers was approaching the crisis.

After my return there followed several weeks of lessened anxiety and of concern with his immediate situation outside of the analysis. He planned to move from a slum tenement to an attractive apartment "in a more respectable part of town." He recognized several difficulties in his job which could be remedied by discussion with his boss; he carried through this discussion to his satisfaction and found increased interest and ambition. He realized new sources of companionship in friends of long standing. His analytic hours were spent in discussing these actual achievements.

Finally, he began a tentative evaluation of my character on a realistic basis, rather than as a representative of the destructive images of his childhood. My personality was discussed very frankly, as it actually is, so far as he knew it.

As a result of this success in facing the realities of his contemporary life, a great sadness and loneliness swept over him; for, at last, he saw in clear outline the hopeless failure of his past years and felt the fear of again failing in the immediate present. This unhappiness was now recognized as having lain beneath his shameful secret and his protective aggressiveness. He had always considered this more tender type of suffering a sign of weakness and had intently avoided it throughout the analysis. Longing for affection, shame, false pride, and hostility he had heretofore succeeded in expressing. Sadness and loneliness had until now been withheld. Their expression represented a new sincerity and directness, and marked a crossway on the road to health.

The sorrowful mood was due, he realized, not only to the early surrender of his own nature but also to his present hopelessness of regaining this lost treasure. He was able at last to acknowledge that he, as well as his parents, had been responsible for the theft. This again increased his shame. He attempted to dispel this familiar, but hitherto unacknowledged, mood of sadness and guilt toward himself by renewed anger at me. I enslaved him. I was in power. He was helpless.

At this time a dream of trying to make his way over a sea of sharp pointed ice represented the painful and difficult personal relation and stimulated a direct storm of hatred at me. Accompanying his anger, however, was a sure knowledge of his need and love for me. The crisis of this conflict ended with a dream of the toppling over of a huge tower. He watched it crash and awoke relieved that such a threatening edifice was destroyed. He now felt "on the level" with me and returned to his realistic evaluation of me and of his own constructive capabilities.

The overthrow of the protective edifice, the tower of his dream, not only enabled him to recognize tentatively his equality with me; it gave him also sufficient strength to allow the deep sense of shame, occasioned by the sordid relationship with his father and the consequent self-destructive way of life, to come more actively to consciousness than heretofore. He admitted for the first time in his life the "loathesome sensations" which he had had as an adolescent boy. This very admission represented to him an exposure to me of his loathesomeness. Yet it was easier even now to remember these feelings of the past than it was to acknowledge that he was actually sensing them as he spoke.

When I mentioned this he became outraged, accused me of

stupidly interrupting his immersion in feeling, and announced that he would never admit that he, in the past or in the present, actually was loathesome. He knew that he had led a life of inferiority to all about him. He had chosen "inferior" occupations, had always been financially dependent on, and sheltered by, relatives and friends, and was again in relation to me dependent. The last step, however, in sensing and acknowledging his present feeling of sordid worthlessness and hopelessness he now defiantly refused to take. Instead he loathed and hated me and said so.

One can see that in this moment of conflict I was actually doing to him what his father had previously done. By my presence in his life as his analyst, I was forcing him to act and feel "loathesome." He was struggling against the admission of such a feeling and was protecting himself from it by fury at me. The difference between the childhood and the analytic situations, however, lay in the fact that his father had pretended to care for him and had in reality done him severe harm; while I had worked constantly and sincerely for several years to help him regain his health and his happiness. And in my own feelings I had respect and admiration for his courageous efforts, his endurance, and his regained integrity. These characteristics in him made him indeed my equal, with the opportunity as well of becoming superior to me.

Such a natural attitude of mind on the part of the analyst, although not always expressed, has a therapeutic effect on the patient in his moments of anguish, for it motivates the analyst's skill and endurance and assists him in presenting the correct and beneficial facet of his own personality to the patient. It can be compared to the proper time exposure of a photographic plate.

The last months of this patient's treatment were given over to his defiant refusal to sense his "loathesomeness" and his shame in his everyday life; to the final admission that this refusal kept him bound to his shameful past; to the gradual humbling and opening of himself to the entrance into consciousness of these deeply repressed sensations of mean enslavement; and to the awareness that he could now start from rock bottom to build an integrated and self-satisfying life.

No longer was he the servant of a cruel father, but was now "master of his fate." He turned first of all to the construction of a new relationship with me, one which could be solid and permanent and in which he was no longer inferior, but free to pursue his aims and ambitions. He was confident that I would not desert him, that I had no wish to do so. He realized a sure desire to show his devotion to me and to be a tribute to our mutual endeavors. As he became increasingly concerned with the satisfying possibilities that life held for him, my part in it grew more shadowy. He was absorbed in living as a person in his own right.

In these latter pages I have followed a patient through the final struggle of his analysis. It can best be described, in his own prognostic words, as "Shame and anger and then love."

In the foregoing examples of psychoanalytic therapy I have attempted to show that the emotional elements underlying neurotic conflict can be reduced to those of anxiety, hatred, and love. A carefully built edifice of protection against their environment and against their own greatly feared passionate impulses can be seen in all persons suffering from neurosis. This edifice is the result of anxious certainty that the environment is hostile and that the inner impulses, in reaction to this hostility, are angry and destructive. As a result, protection takes the form of palliation, conformity, attempts to please, to be "a good child," or, on the contrary, of "orneriness," of dead automatism, and of more unfortunate and destructive character defects.

That this unconscious plan of defense has not succeeded and hence has produced neurotic symptoms is caused by the falsity of the basic illusion, an illusion founded on actual childhood experience but no longer operative in adolescent and adult surroundings. The outcome is the tendency to make enemies or at least to fail in some degree in personal contacts and thus to reproduce the childhood patterns.

In this way the original vicious circle continues and increases the need for defense. Some break in the circle is essential and may be supplied by psychotherapeutic treatment, in which the therapist refuses to become inimical and gives evidence of his friendliness by his tact and skill in assisting the patient to become aware of his protective mechanisms and of the anger that lies beneath them. That hostility on the analyst's part does not result provides the entering wedge and initiates the reversing motion of the patient's emotional motivation.

An unreeling backwards from defense to the anger which caused the defense now follows, and there ensues a period of hostility, combined with anxiety and attempts to revive the defense impulses. The latter grow increasingly weak as anger grows stronger and more direct in verbal expression. Finally, slight signs of tenderness and cooperation are sensed in the patient, accompanied by insight and greater emotional health, both in action and in the birth of constructive wishes. At this point in therapeutic treatment the conflict between the loving impulses, their frustration, the hostile impulses, and anxiety rages unceasingly and is in essence a duplication of childhood experience. This conflict continues to be almost completely based on illusion, for insight is still tentative, and the actual environment, both in and out of the analysis, seems to the patient to be the familiar environment of his youth.

The continuing repetitions of the vicious circle are permanently interrupted by final recognition on the patient's part of the contrast which the analytic situation presents to that of earlier experiences. The analyst has not the personality of the parents nor of their surrogates, the analytic relationship is not at all the same as those of the patient's infancy. In fact, it is completely different; for the analyst in the treatment of his patient has only one aim in view and that is the patient's health and happiness. His patient's protections and hostility do not outrage him. He is only thankful for their expression toward him, and his endeavor is to assist in their understanding. Rationalizations are now of no value; indirection is continually brought to the patient's attention and consciousness; illusions are gradually seen at their face value. The tendency to destroy is found to be useless and is with great relief finally discarded. It is, therefore, inevitable that the rage of hatred gradually, by its expression and its safe outcome, loses its force and is replaced by loving impulses.

To recognize the tenuous separation of hostility from loving-kindness and its expression, and to observe the inevitable rebirth of the tender impulses at the moment when anger changes its course from destruction based on illusion to creative strength in dealing with actuality, enables the psychoanalyst to make a calculated and beneficial use of the two basic emotions and activating principles of human life.

It is in the development and healthy use of love and anger that human beings reach their highest fulfillment. Each of these emotions has its appropriate power, and both should be constructive in expression. It is in their abuse and misuse, which arise in the moral confusion of childhood, that the foundations of neurosis are laid. Hence, it is in the correction of such misapplications and on the growth of these powerful emotions to their rightful and mature expression that psychotherapy bases its various forms of successful treatment.

CHAPTER 4

THE PSYCHOANALYST'S RESPONSE

"Reality between people is the basis of freedom."
—*Freedom in the Modern World.*
JOHN MACMURRAY

THE technical terms "transference" and "counter-transference" represent in the Freudian vocabulary the emotional reactions toward each other of the two persons in the psychoanalytic relationship. And, understood in a broader sense, the phenomenon of transference is constant.[1] It is based on childhood experience, whether wholesome or unwholesome. For, as Freud has made explicit, we are unconsciously reliving throughout our lives, but in adult settings, the emotional experiences of infancy. We find much of our happiness in continuing the successful adaptations and our unhappiness and neurosis in the insistent repetition, often unconscious, of the maladjustments of our unsolved childhood problems. Over these we seem to be compelled to labor, seeking fervently their solution, seeking success in our relations to others. It is these problems which comprise the content of the neurotic person's transference tendencies and that of the neurotic patient's transference during therapy.

The essential purpose of psychoanalytic therapy is to untangle

[1] See above, page 16.

the bewilderment of childhood so that the unhealthy elements of the "repetition compulsion" may be eliminated. The patient learns to comprehend his neurotic phantasy life and in its place to strengthen his sense of reality. The psychotherapeutic situation proves empirically to be dissimiliar to the situation of his earliest years. Therefore his previous defense becomes unavailing and even destructive. He forces himself to cast it aside. As a result he learns for the first time to create a constructive relationship with another person. This becomes his model, in patterns of emotional behavior, for all future relations.

This outcome cannot be achieved by the patient alone. For the word "relationship" presupposes mutuality. There must be at least one other person concerned—in this case, the analyst. It is his own transference to the patient which he contributes to this cooperative enterprise. This provides the realistic foil for the patient's transference phantasies, the screen against which they are projected, the instrument of their calibration. The analyst has himself experienced the process of therapy and has destroyed the neurotic elements in his repetition compulsion. Therefore his transference, the counter-transference, is no longer based on the experiences of his childhood, but on an understanding of these experiences and on the lesson of personal relations learned in his own analysis.

The main distinction between the transference of patient and that of analyst lies in the fact that the latter stems from a greater degree of emotional health and a wider basis of consciousness. He knows himself and can control his conscious expressions. He can be more direct and sincere than the patient, who has come to him for the very reason that he does not know himself.

During treatment the patient unknowingly transfers to the analyst the qualities which he experienced in his childhood as not only those of the significant persons representing to him satisfaction but also of those presenting insoluble problems. At that early period his instinct for self-preservation had unconsciously compelled him to entice his parents by hook or crook to supply his emotional needs, those essential for normal growth. If this proved impossible he created the necessary wish-fulfilling phantasies and by these illusions was thereupon caught in a trap of his own making.

A motherless girl with an exceptionally sadistic father may compulsively choose to devote her childhood to undoing the harm which he is constantly doing to others, by her protection of and comfort to them, submitting herself to his cruelty without complaint. The basis of this behavior is the phantasy that her father is not cruel but is the loving parent whom she needs in order to persist. She has, however, always known in her heart that he actually was a terrifying and threateningly harmful figure. Both her sense of reality and her phantasies operate to preserve her sanity. If she had given herself up to phantasy she would have eventually become psychotic. If reality had been entirely accepted she would have perished from lack of emotional nourishment. Therefore it was essential to keep both tendencies functioning. They are, however, in eternal conflict; and this conflict creates a further compulsion. She must eventually solve the new problem, she must somehow get herself out of this trap, she must prevent herself from being crushed and destroyed between the two opposing forces. Her self-preservative instinct again comes to the fore, but in a new form. By way of the repetition compulsion she unconsciously dedicates her life to an attempt to solve the struggle between phantasy and reality. Was he in fact the cruelly dominating father or the loving father for whom she longed? In endeavoring to answer this insistent question, the early enigmatic paternal personage must be envisaged in each person who assumes importance to her in her later life. She must use each one as a battleground, continually and anxiously trying to force him to be a loving parent and to give her what she has always needed and still needs. In this effort she inevitably fails, for no one can be found who duplicates her father's personality and hence she cannot successfully force some substitute father to reform and become the longed-for parent. Nor can she superimpose upon others the figure of her father and his arbitrary cruelty, without creating enemies. This program, therefore, initiated in her childhood, can only result in unsuccessful personal relations, in continual unhappiness; and it ends in neurosis.

At birth the infant is confronted with three varying sets of emotional circumstances: his individual temperament, the product of his vast heredity; his impulse to grow to maturity, the passionate substance of which is individual in quantity; and the nature and character of those persons who are in intimate contact with him. It is this last factor which forms the parents' responsibility. It should produce an attitude and behavior on their part which can be called a cherishing love.

A love that cherishes is a love that seeks empathically to comprehend another's individual temperament and individual needs; one that in essence sufficiently respects the feeling life and passionate nature of the other person to allow him their full expression and development; one that refrains from intruding upon the precious privacy of another's mental and emotional existence. Rainer Maria Rilke expressed this succinctly: "But once the realization is accepted that even between the *closest* human beings infinite distances continue to exist, a wonderful living side by side can grow up, if they succeed in loving the distance between them which makes it possible for each to see the other whole and against a wide sky!" Such an ideal is difficult for human beings to attain. But it can be approached. The nearer the approach, the healthier the loved one's environment; the healthier the child who is exposed; and in psychotherapy, the more beneficial is the effect upon the patient.

This essential therapeutic setting delineates in the large the scope of the counter-transference. The therapist must cherish his patient, must labor for the recovery of his characteristic nature and for its growth and maturity. He must respect his patient's emotional temperament and its expression. He must provide a secure scene for such expression. He must recognize incontrovertibly that his patient is trying with all his power to become a person who meets with his own inner approval and respect; a person who is capable of judging himself with moral truth; a person who will and can endure the disillusion of facing his own sense of morality, his "inner voice."

Within this broad outline are the detailed expressions of the counter-transference. These vary with each patient and each analyst. Nor can they be decided upon at the beginning of treatment. They evolve during the growing familiarity with the patient's life history, with his true nature and its potentialities, and with the various personality traits which have developed in reaction to an oppressing environment, in particular that of his childhood; such traits as, for example, submission, rebellion, vengefulness, and an impelling eagerness to identify oneself with others. These traits are easily recognized as being exaggerated in expression and as being protections in some form against the early all-powerful surroundings. They are known as "defense mechanisms." As the patient's innate character structure gradually becomes evident, these mechanisms are seen to be entirely inappropriate.

The spoken story of the patient's life is necessarily distorted by his childhood conflicts, which are still in operation. It is essential to examine this at its face value and to respect it as the product of his self-preservation. It must also be constantly viewed and measured in comparison with his behavior, both outside the analyst's office and toward the analyst himself. This behavior includes not only external acts but dreams and phantasies, and the recognition and expression of emotions. It forms the dynamic content of the patient's transference. It proceeds by leaps and bounds, turning and twisting as he unconsciously imagines the analyst to represent the puzzling figures of his childhood; and as he attempts to force him out of these roles and into the desired figure of the longed-for parent.

The analyst in reaction to this shifting activity must maintain two attitudes. He must endeavor with full sympathy to recognize and then to describe in his own words the patient's self-portrait which is being drawn, even in its distortions; and, second, he must allow himself in its regard whatever expression of his own realistic and moral point of view is for the benefit of the sufferer. Both attitudes represent the counter-transference. The former represents, in its emotional comprehension, its general scope; the latter, its details. The former must pervade every analytic treatment regardless of the analyst's temperament; the latter must also be constantly present but its form of expression is entirely dependent upon the analyst's temperament and character. It is indeed the expression, in reaction to each differing patient, of the analyst's nature as it has emerged through his own therapeutic analysis. Hence the detailed content of the counter-transference varies, but it is always based on the analyst's basic character structure and on his desire to be the parent who would have insured the normal development of the patient when a child.

One of the adventures of being a psychotherapist lies in the opportunity to express beneficially one's true nature, one's true feelings and ideas, in reaction to each phase of the patient's therapy and to each facet of personality which the patient exposes, whether neurotic and defensive or courageous and direct. Each such adventure is completely different from every other, as no two patients are in any way similar. The analyst cannot know at the beginning of treatment just how the therapeutic course will run. That he should decide to elicit from the patient a given type of transference, or choose his own type of counter-transference for the benefit of the patient, seems a wholly misguided form of manipulation, out of line with the reality of successful personal relationships. It is essential that the analyst bide his time and that he observe what course the patient himself will present. In reaction to the patient's own program, the counter-transference will develop its own appropriate expression. Therefore, the sense of adventure.

As examples of counter-transference, I offer the following two instances:

1. The child whom I mentioned earlier came to me as a patient fifty years of age, married to a lawyer of distinction, and with two sons. Although she and her husband had formerly consulted me about one of her sons, she had gone to another analyst for a few months work on her own problems. Due to unavoidable circumstances he had referred her to me for the continuance of her work. At the time when she and her husband had consulted me, I had been impressed by the husband's aggressive assumption of the lead and by her submission to this.

My first impression of her was of a withdrawn personality. But my curiosity was evoked by her sensitivity. In reaction to this attitude of mine, acutely sensed by her, she had told her analyst that she feared she could not work with me because of my coldness and of her anxiety that, sharing the same social background, I probably knew many of her relatives and friends. Her analyst, however, persuaded her to make the attempt. She came to her first therapeutic interview with apparent enthusiasm. I noticed, however, that she referred frequently to her former analyst, a European by origin, quoting with admiration many of his technical expressions. As our conversation developed I observed her insight into her own childhood situation and into her immediate problems.

She had written notes of her ideas. These were startlingly succinct and clear. In contrast, her method of speech, in a high, complaining, and frantic voice, was filled with politenesses and with indefinite terms. There was nothing I could put my finger on. My suggestion that she seemed to be in a panic succeeded in calming her and she proceeded to tell me the story of her childhood. It had been divided between a cruel, dominating but fascinatingly seductive father, a Russian professor, and her dead mother's New England family of high social standing. Both sides of her family had been strict conformists in their own tradition and each had had entirely different ideas of conformity. She gave as an example the differing table manners. When with her father, she had been trained to use both fork and knife together in the European way; when with the New England grandmother, she had been taught to transfer her fork from the left to the right hand. She became adept at this constant change of custom, submitting with no thought of rebellion. Indeed she developed an exaggerated sense of loyalty to both sides of her family and hence forced herself to accept the idiosyncrasies of each. This demanded unusual self-control, in reality a denial of herself and of her own values.

On a small scale this symbolic experience was being re-enacted in her situation with me. She had accustomed herself to her former analyst and had learned by rote his technically worded interpretations. She was now in a panic as she watched my different manners and methods. She often unconsciously reproved me for not being more technical; but when I suggested that she missed in me this manner of speech, she hurriedly denied my suggestion. Here again she was trying to adjust successfully to two differing situations, trying to be loyal to each. There was no recognition in her of her own preferences and desires. I wondered how to allay her anxiety of loyalty, so that she could tell me more of her terrifying life under her cruel father's domination; of her happier but sterile life with her New England grandmother. She began her story by explaining her childhood in her former analyst's terms. I suggested that she try to recall the emotions of those early days rather than to interpret them. Panic again raised its head. I seemed to be asking her to deny her loyalty to her other analyst.

A chance was given me to correct her phantasies about me when she suggested that I must know members of her mother's family, that I was probably a New Englander. I then told her in detail of my immediate ancestry; that I had not been brought up in New England; and that, although I had chanced to meet a few members of her family, I did not know them well. I did, however, know a good deal about them, so that anything she told me would not surprise me. This willingness to tell her of myself formed the entering wedge to break her anxiety, so that we could begin on a more equal footing. I was neither a European nor a New Englander of distinction. From a snobbish point of view, I could be considered a nobody. She confessed that she herself as a child had felt an outsider with both sides of her family. She was never really admitted nor wanted by either. Hence her determined loyalty to both was seen as a bribe for admission. This confession gave me the opportunity to suggest that we must find out who she really was and is. If neither a foreigner of renown nor a New Englander of social consequence, who then is she?

In this instance of the functioning of the counter-transference we see the attempt on my part to discredit the patient's endeavor to transfer her lifelong emotional reactions upon me. The patient has reacted to her two analysts as if one were a representation of her father, the other, of her grandmother. In either case she is on familiar ground, although filled with anxious compulsion to be loyal and self-denying. My assertion that I belonged to neither category filled her with the anxiety of unfamiliarity. On the other hand it placed me in her own company and in alliance with herself. I, too, have known Europeans and New Englanders, but as an outsider. It can be surmised that she, in identifying me with herself, will attempt to discipline me as she was once disciplined and as she now disciplines herself and hence will treat me in a superior manner; first as if she were a distinguished foreigner and then as if she were a New Englander born and bred. It is probable that I will not condone her patronizing attitude, but instead will show her her own false identification with both sides of her family. This will demand from me a tactful support of my system of values as against those of her father and of her grandmother, as voiced by her; and it will reawaken in her her childhood wish to have done likewise. It will encourage her to find and develop her own sense of values which lies silently beneath her constant efforts to appease.

At the beginning of treatment the counter-transference is thus seen to be exercised with "gloved hands," gently and tentatively, in accordance with the patient's ability and unconscious willingness to accept as an important figure one who refuses to fit into his transference compulsion. Sufficient time must always be given the expression of this compulsion so that the patient's emotional reactions to his childhood figures can be vented. The fact that, in response, he does not suffer reproval nor rejection from the analyst surprises and encourages him. It is at these points in treatment that the analyst can discuss frankly the patient's transference, either admitting its correctness or suggesting its incorrectness. This discussion is not authoritatively maintained but offered as an opinion. As a result the patient's compulsion is temporarily eased, and his anxiety relieved. For it is probable that all anxiety stems from an unconscious dread that human beings really are as all-powerful, unloving, and untrustworthy as were those of childhood, and that the repetition compulsion of the neurosis—the compelling need to substitute a phantastic environmental scene, similar to that of childhood, for the actual contemporary scene—must not be given up but must be continued in desperate self-protection.[2] This would mean the hopelessness of the tempting therapeutic relationship, which is often the last hope. That the patient's transference can be discussed dispassionately by the analyst must at least mean that if it is factual, it is not dangerous.

2. At a later stage in therapy when the patient has gained greater emotional strength, he benefits by a less gentle expression of the counter-transference—one that is "straight from the shoulder," not so much as if he were an ailing person.

An instance of this is seen in a patient, a young worker in the Y.M.C.A., who suffered the effects of a long childhood under an extremely sadistic father and a weak, hypocritical mother. No natural impulse was allowed expression, except by his mother behind his father's back. By this father he was horsewhipped, tongue-lashed, and humiliated with ridicule. Born with a passionate nature, excellent mentality, and a rich capacity for the enjoyment of life he survived his evil infantile experiences. To do this he created a sentimental and false idealism as a safe rationalization of his angry rebellion.

In the first period of his treatment he presented these ideals

[2] See "Anxiety," p. 133.

of conformity in an aggressive and bombastic manner. He blew his own horn with defiance; but at the same time he insisted, also with defiance, that he needed to take notes on my "pearls of wisdom," for fear that he would forget them. This carried out his father's frequent reproof: "Your ignorance is only exceeded by your impudence!" Because of this admonishment he had originated a clever and quick method of sizing up all situations involving others. An acute intuitive sense, often combined with sarcasm, allowed him to use this criterion aggressively. As a result he tended to make enemies of all who held positions of power; to convert them willy-nilly into symbols of his cruel father. In contrast to this, he had no hostile inclination toward those who were less important than himself. He was an excellent teacher. In this manifestation he unconsciously showed his father what a good parent should be.

Because he came to me for help, he hoped that I would be this beneficent parent and would believe in his idealistic rationalizations. They were all he had to offer. At first I felt respect for them, for I knew that they stemmed from something of value in his personality. They were, however, so unrealistic and defiant that I could not tolerate them for long. I found it essential, for my own honesty, to point this out to him. With this admonition I became for him the cruel parent. His manner toward me changed radically and for several months he was the impudent child, so despised by his father. But I did not despise him. I recognized in his behavior his rebellion against what he considered his domination by me. He proceeded to fight me tooth and nail, but never directly. He finally succeeded in vanquishing me, by making me powerless to help him. I could not withstand his quick wit, his cruelly underhand attacks. I was worn down and saddened by his meanness. I finally told him that in this mood he seemed obnoxious to me. He could not believe that I could be so severely critical. Nor could he believe that he had overpowered me. I explained, however, that he made me powerless and confessed that I could see no way of helping him. I explained that because he tired me out, emotionally and physically, I would have to end the treatment.

Needless to say I did not feel that I was rejecting him but that his neurosis had conquered me. This was for him, however, a complete rejection and was at once followed by great anxiety. His defensive aggression had gone too far, it had got out of hand; and he was the victim, rather than I. His genuine hopelessness made me reconsider my decision and offer to continue our work for a short trial period. We saw together how powerfully he functioned when under his protective compulsion of hostility, and that in the previous months his attempt had been to test my power, which he feared, and to force me to admit my weakness. In this attempt he had succeeded. Symbolically speaking, he had brought his father to his knees.

Having reached this climax with me, he was able to see that in all his contacts with those in positions superior to himself he reacted in the same manner. Initially he defiantly asserted his excellent capacities, shouting his idealism from the housetops. When this made but little impression he became impudently rebellious. Because of his fear of authority, his rebellion took an indirect and cowardly route. Both his defiance and his rebellion aroused inimical reactions in others, threatening rejection. At this point he would be overcome with anxiety, admitting to himself defeat and worthlessness. Thus ran the cycle from defiant superiority to anxious inferiority. The net result was a constant dread, and often a conviction that each person in power was a potential enemy and might well plot against him for his eventual destruction.

This neurotic way of life symbolized accurately the content of his emotional reactions to his parents during his early years. This fact became clearly recognizable. We were able to picture his attempt, as a child, to assert his true nature; his defiance at its cruel rejection by his father; the replacement of his defiance with a system of idealistic rationalizations, due probably to the effect of his mother's hypocrisy. These ideals were safe from ridicule. They would doubtless evoke respect, for they were many times based on phrases from the Bible—quotations which he knew by heart. With the belittling of his excellent mind by his father came the development of a quick wit and an unbearable impudence. This was for the purpose of taunting in revenge, at least in phantasy. Accompanying this meanness was the unconscious fear of exposure, revealing his worthlessness and powerlessness.

At each step of the treatment he unconsciously transferred upon me the emotional attitudes of his father. He could not see me nor comprehend me in reality. I, as myself, did not exist for him. In me his father must be destroyed. But when he succeeded in overwhelming me myself, and not his father, and in forcing me to admit my impotence, my inability to help him, he found himself in danger of losing the good parent for whom he had hoped and whom he had always needed. His anxiety at this threatened loss temporarily broke the compulsion, and there ensued a period of insight.

This outcome would not have been possible without the expression of the counter-transference. From the beginning of therapy I freely reacted to the varying indications of his repetition compulsion, as he exposed them. I admired and had trust in the assets which he seemed to possess. When he boasted of his idealism, however, I showed my belief that he was unsure of these assets. When he defended himself with defiance and mean cruelty, I accused him of these destructive tendencies.

When he attempted to trick me into submission, I confessed my impotence, as well as my sorrow that I had not succeeded in helping him. With the crumbling of his compulsion and the exposure of his anxiety, I offered to try again. These expressions stemmed from my sincere attitude at each point of the cycle. That they helped him to insight and to a new sense of reality was due to the fact that he was not treated by me as his father had treated him, but with an honest and kindly hope of being of benefit and with the recognition of him as an individual.

Throughout treatment the analyst must sense the exact moments when a critical appraisal of the patient's phantasies and behavior, either encouraging or discouraging, is needed. That this should never be hostile goes without saying. The aim of these expressions of the counter-transference is always that of the patient's health. How much admiration can he stand? How much disapproval? Surrounding these appraisals must always be the respect due him for his present attempt to become a healthy and happy person.

The patient's transference is "countered" as an essential element in analytic therapy, by the analyst's counter-transference. This is a central factor in the process of exposing the patient's unconscious childhood illusions to his adult reality. Toward the conclusion of treatment, when the neurotic symptoms have been discarded and the infantile phantasies have worn away, one task remains unfinished: that of assisting the patient to apply his maturing sense of reality to his own personality and to that of his analyst.

In this undertaking he takes stock of his earlier frequent attempts to force illusory roles upon the analyst. That he has never succeeded in these attempts is due to the fact that his analyst has not only given him insight into such behavior but has also unhesitatingly exposed his own nature in so far as this can be of benefit. This continuing exposure, because so closely interwoven with the discarding of the illusions, has not attained any real substance for the patient. It has assumed a negative rather than a positive aspect. He can enumerate the characteristics which the analyst does *not* possess—as, for example, those of the significant persons of his childhood. He is aware of only a few which he possesses. These are generalized qualities, such as patience, kindness, endurance or forgetfulness, unpunctuality and self-interest. But just who he is, what kind of temperament he has, what interests he has, what are his more profound assets and liabilities—these are questions that must now be answered by the patient's realistic observation.

He is simultaneously asking the same questions about his own personality; for he has discovered that he has known himself, up to the present moment, no better than he knew his analyst.

During this later period of questioning the patient has, with his other symptoms, discarded the neurotic elements in his transference. If he were still laboring under the repetition compulsion, he would not be in quest of his analyst's personality. He would delude himself into thinking that he is entirely familiar with all his guises. But now he admits that he hardly knows him at all. He still tries halfheartedly to find similarities between his analyst and the figures of his childhood. Finally he admits his failure and at last attempts to make his acquaintance. This is accomplished as in the forming of firm friendship: by discussions on the many subjects that are now of interest to the patient; by questions and answers about specific human relations, including the analyst's relation to him, and about human relations in general.

The analyst realizes that the patient's concern is not so much in detailed answers as in the general atmosphere of intimate kindliness. He wishes to feel the analyst's trust in him, to know that the analyst will not answer any questions which are too private. The fact that the analyst answers some and not others gives him confidence. He foresees a time when he will maintain his own privacy, too, from this friend. But for these last weeks there is nothing that cannot be talked over in some degree or form. Gradually the patient gains a more realistically detailed picture of his analyst and of himself. And, as in friendship, with greater intimacy there grows a deepening affection. This is an entirely new experience, for failure in human relations has been his greatest liability.

As the patient pursues this experiment in friendship, his transference tendencies represent a true expression of his emotional health. The analyst also is now free to exercise his full transference to the patient. He is free to respond to this offer of friendship, to evaluate with admiration the courageous effort of his patient during the past years, to admit that he will miss their companionship, and to thank him for the happiness which the patient's health now gives him. In thus accepting his share of this new and mature intimacy the analyst becomes in reality the parent necessary to the health and happiness of all children. He has given this child the strength and freedom to leave him and to go out into the world to seek his fortune.

Freud has defined conclusively the extended operations of the repetition compulsion in human existence. Human beings are concerned constantly with the joys and sorrows of their childhood. Indeed we feel ourselves to be in essence the child of our memories. The phenomenon of transference is the product of this compulsion, the expression of its content. We unconsciously compel each person of our later life to represent the important figures of our earliest days, so that we can relive our moments of greatest intensity.

It remained for Ferenczi to show that the illusions of childhood, its moral confusion and its unsolved problems, could only be dispelled in the presence and with the aid of a true parental substitute. This substitute must be by nature and in expression the all-embracing mother, "Thalassa."[3] The more accurately the parent-therapist supplies the needs of emotional growth in the patient, the more complete the cure.

This theory brought to the fore the significance of the counter-transference. It stressed the fact that it is the most essential tool of the therapist: one that must arise from his innate temperament, and one that is solely concerned with the patient's recovery of emotional health.

Developing the initial contribution of Ferenczi to this subject, it can be stated that the counter-transference in psychoanalytic therapy may now be recognized as differing only in goal from the same factor in other personal relations. The actual dynamics are those of all successful human relationships, whether of two friends, of two lovers, or of mother and child.

The essential characteristic of the counter-transference is one of tenderness. In the fact that the patient is at first emotionally unstable, unsuccessful in his pursuit of happiness, and in dire need of assistance, he is still the confused child of his early years. In contradistinction the analyst is the mature parent. He offers a setting of security and warmth, in which the patient by means of his varying expressions in transference exposes the unsolved problems of his infancy.

The content of the counter-transference changes with the improving health of the patient. From the careful and sympathetic study and observation at the beginning of treatment, to the more matter-of-fact, meticulous, and empathic examination of the

[3] *Thalassa: A Theory of Genitality*, by Sándor Ferenczi, Psychoanalytic Quarterly, Inc., New York, 1938.

patient's phantasies and behavior in a later period, it progresses to the final "give and take" with the patient, as a person of equal emotional vigor.

One thinks of many instances in childhood which are a condensation of this lengthy process of therapy. A child may come running to his mother's arms, screaming hysterically. She holds him tenderly and firmly, quieting him with loving words, wondering what has occasioned his terror. As the sobbing ceases, she asks him what is wrong. In the comfort of her embrace he tells her, at first falteringly and then in a passionate outburst. His hurt pride, his anger, his confusion pour out. Little by little she is able to make suggestions, to point out his misconceptions and the mistakes that he has made. Because of his trust in her he can accept her reproofs, can agree with some of her ideas and refuse others. They can then settle down together to a quiet "talking it all over," in which the child regains his lost self-confidence. No longer is he the sobbing child running to his mother's shelter. No longer does he need to hear her words of comfort. He is now impatient to be away upon new adventures, safe in the knowledge of her sure comradeship.

The constant repetition of such experiences in infancy and, on a more mature level, in later childhood and adolescence, makes for a wholesome emotional life in adulthood. If the child has lacked this wise parent, and hence has become neurotic, psychotherapy must offer as its primary gift the needed parental substitute. This demands an embracing atmosphere of loving-kindness. It demands no less the honest expression of the psychotherapist's attitudes toward the patient's varying transference productions and toward the ripening of his true nature. These must arise from one source only, the sincere and ardent desire to bring the patient to emotional maturity.

Chapter 5

RECONCILIATION: A CREATIVE ACHIEVEMENT

Disharmony is for human beings unendurable.[1]

Human infants, with few exceptions, are born into the possession of a loving environment. This is a continuance of the wholesome uterine existence. It may, in misfortune, last but a few days or months. It represents the "security" which our modern pediatricians, psychotherapists, and sociologists impress upon us as necessary to a child's health of body, mind, and spirit. These specialists in human relations often say, in one way or another, "Children must be given love—or else . . ."—tending to frighten beneficent parents. Yet surely they must know that love, of all things, cannot be given in answer to warnings.

They insist that love is essential to growth, but sometimes they fail to make clear the one most significant reason for this fact—a reason which they may consider self-evident: that to be surrounded by cherishing care allows and calls forth the response of love from the baby. It is this response, this extension of the baby's self, which is of fundamental importance as motivation to each physiological system in his body, as well as to the mental and emotional areas of his personality. Doctors C. Anderson Aldrich

[1] Quoted from Dr. Otto Kant, in personal conversation.

and Mary M. Aldrich, in *Babies Are Human Beings*, say that at no time of life does the human being make such strenuous effort as in infancy. "He goes at his job in an intensely serious way." If we are unable to consider the growing process to be purely automatic, we must seek an emotional motivation for this earliest serious endeavor.

It is my belief that this motivation can be found in the infant's own need to love, to love himself in loving all who surround him. His every effort is outgoing; he becomes larger, in every sense of the word, from the moment of conception. He grows outward into the environment, taking up more and more space, coming into closer and closer contact with each detail of his surroundings. From the point of view of his emotional development the most important of such details are the human beings who are nearest to him. He extends himself toward them. This extension of himself in love provides the stimulus for the child's wholesome development of mind and body. It is the dynamo that transforms his energy. To secure this extension for the child, the environment must provide an embracing atmosphere, the baby must be loved. By this gift of love the baby is assured of the opportunity to develop and to express his innate capacity and longing to *give* love, and so to create in himself the emotional stimulus basic to healthy growth. As we well know, the act of loving stimulates one's whole being. The emotion of love vitalizes each physical and mental process.

There are few parents who cannot accept these fundamental facts and who cannot lovingly endeavor to provide this opportunity. The inherent temperament of the infant, however, in his very growth soon places stumbling blocks in the path of the mutual relationship with those around him. Growth is a passionate process, as the Aldriches make clear, and implies a developing according to one's own inherited constitution. It is ruthless in its intensity; and hence, sooner or later, it runs counter to the wishes and demands of the human environment, as well as to the laws of the physical world. The security which surrounds the baby may be, as a result, slowly, or on occasion suddenly, withdrawn.

In some cases the infant's nature in conjunction with the temperaments of his parents makes inevitable this blockage, often resulting in disastrous character deformation. In other cases it may be that external circumstances produce this unfortunate effect—as in the case of a two-year-old boy, whose younger and only sister was born with a clubfoot. This little boy suffered a traumatic rejection by his parents in favor of his sister. A thwarting block was erected in the path of his healthful development. It was then essential for him unconsciously to devise a new path of growth; for life persists, whether moving forward or backward or at a tangent. A neurotic organization—or, as Dr. Andras Angyal defines it,[2] "a neurotic way of life"—was established by this child, and a severely distorted personality was put into process throughout his early years, continuing into adulthood.

There is in all human experience, and at an early age, a traumatic moment, or a series of such moments, in which the significant human figures are at serious odds with the child. It is then that the basic need of the child to express his love, and so to stimulate his wholesome growth processes, experiences at the least a loss of nourishment, at the most a cruel frustration, a harsh stoppage. This moment represents "disharmony" and is unendurable to the child.

If disharmony is unendurable to human beings, an attempt must always be made to undo the harmful condition. Here the

[2] "The Convergence of Psychotherapy and Religion," *Journal of Pastoral Care,* Vol. 5, No. 4, Winter, 1952.

need for reconciliation comes into play. Reconciliation is defined as "restoration to harmony or friendship." And this is exactly what the infant or young child attempts to do. His need to love is so imperative that he is unconsciously willing to sacrifice his own nature in order to yield his will to that of his parents, to learn how to become the child whom they will accept with love. No effort is too great to achieve the restoration of this friendship, to again find value in his parents' eyes. His behavior, the nature of his thought processes, his standards of value, even the choice of what emotions to allow into consciousness and to express, gradually become the basis of his re-formed personality. He may lose all originality of thought and of imagination; he may become an unfeeling person, almost totally devitalized; he may suffer from chronic psychosomatic illness. This change of personality in many cases forms the initial step in the structuring of a neurosis, "a consistent process with its own logic and laws," as it is described by Dr. Angyal.

The two-year-old boy mentioned above learned from his tragic rejection to base his entire behavior and eventually his moral principles upon the standards of his parents: as, for example, that the one crime to be avoided was that of "hurting the feelings" of another person. In his case, this meant the hurting of his sister's feelings and, more important, those of his mother, who with exaggerated sensitivity believed that she, and she alone, was responsible for her daughter's deformity. Trained never to hurt the feelings of another, he was forced to practice deception, to lie and to steal. His natural curiosity was diverted into voyeurism. His mental equipment, of unusual caliber, was channeled in early adulthood into the solving of narrowly technical problems in the fields of human communication and propaganda. He suffered from sexual impotence and from an inability to sense in himself either anger or love. His emotional life, what little there was of it, was devoted to long associations with difficult personalities, whom he wooed and studied assiduously, attempting, but without success, to communicate with them, to adjust to their neurotic complications. He had created for himself a sterile life.

The human need for reconciliation can thus be seen to be one origin of neurosis. It comes to light again when the neurosis is full-blown and the sufferer is finally forced to admit his need for help. For here the primary difficulty is always and inevitably one of unhappy, unsuccessful personal relations. There is no neurotic sufferer who is not to a large extent incapable of living at peace and in loving-kindness with his fellow men. This is the very core of his neurosis. This is his basic complaint when he asks for psychotherapeutic assistance. Again he seeks to become reconciled; he seeks harmonious relationships with the significant figures of his environment.

Having in his childhood sacrificed his true nature in order to regain the friendship of his parents, the neurotic has continued along the unwholesome tangential path of development upon which he then embarked. His innate temperament in later years increasingly suffers distortion, in the belief and hope that all people with whom he comes in close contact will be consistent with those of his childhood to whom he had attempted to adjust —that they will make the same demands, will accept his constant endeavor to yield to their wishes, and will at long last love him in return for his self-sacrifice. The unhappiness that has always accompanied this unavailing sacrifice, the sense of self-blame and the unconscious guilt for the treason to his real self have, however, constantly prevented his earning the longed-for acceptance. For in the development of his neurosis he has become an unloving person, impossible to love in return. This is paradoxically a repetition of the early experience of failure, when he initially forced himself to forsake his true path of growth.

The great sacrifice, made as a little child, has not succeeded; for in his urgent need to be loved so that in turn he might extend himself in love, he has compelled himself to proceed along his chosen neurotic pathway through adolescence and adulthood. The constant experience of failure finally overcomes him and, admitting the disharmony of his life, he asks for help. Each neurotic patient asks the same kind of questions: "How can I succeed in friendship? How can I restore, how can I learn to nourish, my personal relationships? I'm at my wit's end in my relation to my children, my spouse, my friends, my boss!"

The third appearance of the need for reconciliation comes during successful psychotherapeutic treatment and in a new form. In contradistinction to its motivation in the creation of neurosis and to its motivation in seeking therapeutic aid, we now find it as one of the final signs of "cure."

The psychotherapeutic process is one of establishing for the first time in the patient's life a successful and enduring personal relationship. It consists of a joint study by patient and therapist of the patient's character distortions as they are seen in their incipience in early childhood, as they have compulsively developed throughout the patient's later years, and as they are expressed in the patient's experience during therapy, both in his external environment and in increasing intensity toward the therapist himself in the transference phenomena. These distortions do, in fact, in the process of therapy wear themselves thin. They are powerless in accomplishing their neurotic goal; for, being distortions, the therapist learns to penetrate their disguise and refuses to yield to their pressure. If he should accept with open arms the false image, as if it were true, he proves to the patient that he cannot lovingly accept his true nature. This would be the triumph which the neurosis had attempted to bring about. If he refuses to accept the false image, not acknowledging it as a self-preservative effort of the rejected child, he behaves exactly as did the childhood figures, who loved neither the false nor the true image. This result would repeat the failures of his neurotic personal relations. The former outcome would represent to the patient his final and conclusive acceptance as a distorted personality; the latter would represent the now familiar failures. By refusing to play the patient's unconscious game with his character distortions, the therapist places essential emphasis on the value of the patient's nature, which is hidden beneath these distortions. In this refusal he also shows respect for the patient's early insistence on saving his life although at the risk of losing his integrity—and perhaps his sanity.

The final stage in psychotherapy is a period of research in seeking to become reconciled. The many unsuccessful relationships of the patient's former life are passed in review, are examined and re-evaluated. An attempt is made with fresh eyes and maturing emotions to put the blame where it belongs. Soon it becomes manifest that this is fruitless; that this is indeed out of line with the longing to develop in loving-kindness. Forgiveness of the mistakes in the tragic past becomes a needed expression of love. And, with forgiveness, the past is recognized in a new light. In the newly recovered endeavor to live lovingly with one's parents, with all the significant figures of one's childhood—if only in memory—and with one's self, the patient becomes aware that in all human beings there is true goodness: what the Quakers call "that of God in every man." The same train of emotional events takes place in regard to contemporary relationships and, last of all, in regard to the therapist. Here mistakes and misunderstandings, by both therapist and patient, over the long period of therapy, are mutually admitted, regretted, and forgiven. True reconciliation is thereby achieved.

The success long sought, of learning to restore friendship in full independence, makes possible the recapturing of one's own inner self. In extending one's self in loving-kindness according to one's true nature, one creates that very environment of love which in turn invites the continuing fulfillment of one's loving potentialities.

PART II. *Dynamic Constants in Psychoneurosis*

Chapter 6

ANXIETY

In the course of psychotherapeutic treatment anxiety is constantly present. In this constancy it differs from other neurotic symptoms, which appear and disappear in the varying expressions of the patient's emotional conflicts. In the phenomenon of transference these conflicts exist between patient and therapist. But whatever the changing forms of other neurotic symptoms, anxiety is a continuous accompaniment. No psychotherapeutic interview is without this symptom, whether admitted by the patient or recognized in its unconscious manifestation by the therapist.

It is thus essential that the therapist attempt to understand the nature of anxiety. How and when did it arise? What is its dynamic basis? What purpose, if any, did it originally serve, does it now serve? How can the patient be relieved of this burden?

Anxiety is not an emotion in itself. We can speak of love, jealousy, fear, or anger as emotions. We cannot so speak of anxiety. Yet anxiety unquestionably has an emotional content; we *feel* anxious. But it is as an adverb to a verb: we may feel anxiously whether we love, are jealous, are fearful, or are angry. It is a feeling tone, not in itself a feeling. It may accompany emotions of whatever kind; and it is a constant element in those who are its victims, no matter what emotion they are experiencing.

Anxiety is often confused with the emotion of fear and yet they are not synonymous. For fear, as I understand the term, means a justifiable apprehension, and it does have a direct factual causation. If we have abdominal pain we are afraid of ulcers or of an inflamed appendix, either of which conditions could be true. When a cyclone is approaching, we fear for the destruction of ourselves or of our home. If a beloved one is uncontrollably jealous or angry, we fear for his sanity and for our happiness.

Fear is realistic, demanding action on our part in response, in order to save ourselves or others. Anxiety is unrealistic, asking in response only that active attention on the part of others be paid to it. Unlike fear it does not demand that its possessor rearrange his situation for its relief; for its chief characteristic is impotence. Its expression may be thus paraphrased: "I am worried and helpless. I don't know what to do in this situation. *You* must help me."

How does this all-pervading sensation arise in human beings? It must at some moment have had an actual basis. It must have been caused by a real experience—one in which the person was in fact impotent, in which he could not assert his own power but had to rely on the power of others. This impotence can only stem from early childhood; for at no other time in life is there such disparity in power, whether physical or emotional or both, as exists between parents and their young children.

In some instances, within a few days or months succeeding birth, the love and security that the infant has learned to expect may be withdrawn. Accompanying such insecurity there must arise confusion and anxiety. That which should be present for the gratifying experience of growth is absent. As the months pass, the self-absorption of unloving parents often makes it impossible to arouse their attention except by the victim's condition of helplessness, drawn to their notice by innumerable worryful signs and symptoms.

We are assisted in our understanding of the condition of anxiety by recognizing that, since it arose from factual experience and succeeded in gaining its hoped-for results, it is certain to continue as a compensating and safeguarding activity. Originally the gratification of being attended to was at least obtained, although in lieu of affectionate concern; and therefore, as in all cases of phantastic production, the basis was one of actuality. The primary phantasy might be expressed in this suppositious form: "If only life were not like this, I would be safe and happy. It seems to be this way; but perhaps I am seeing it incorrectly. I hope so. But it does give me this impression and so I must protect myself in case it really is as it seems." This phantasy gives evidence of complete confusion and of the constantly increasing need to balance probabilities and improbabilities against each other. Such balancing is permeated by the timid hope that these evaluations may be incorrect and unnecessary. This is further evidence of the helplessness of the unloved child. In this intricate play of uncertainties we see the initial steps in the building of neurosis with its accompaniment of anxiety.

The actions of parents are often inconsistent with their words —indeed in exact opposition. The child cannot fathom this confusing paradox. His inclination is to play safe in response to their behavior. He would choose to trust in their expressions of affection, whether in act or in word; but, after all, his world is one of action, not of words. Parents do not often act lovingly toward their children while at the same time openly admitting their *lack* of love for them. It is, however, a frequent experience for a child to be treated cruelly and yet told in the next breath that this treatment is for his good and because he is loved. If the parents thus assert their love for him in words alone, his need is split in two: (1) to be secure in face of unloving behavior, and (2) to believe that his parents are as loving and understanding as they say they are. Such inconsistency and insincerity is the main enigma of childhood. No matter what the child's empirical judgment may decide, he is inevitably in an uncertain and anxious state.

In this destructive environment of confusion the child has two choices of reaction. On the one hand, he may choose to abide by his parents' words and to discount their unloving behavior. In this case he refuses to trust their actions, he insists to himself that they mean what they say. Hence he must protect himself by an inner structure. He must force himself to believe the words which are unsupported by his experience. He must put his faith in his phantastic wishes. This is a decisive element in the incidence of actual psychosis. Accompanying it is the worry that the immersion in wish-fulfilling phantasy is baseless; that he is in greater danger from his parents' acts than he acknowledges. Anxiety therefore invades his life of phantasy.

On the other hand, the child may choose to save himself in the face of hostile behavior, no matter how loving the verbal expression. This is a decisive element in the incidence of neurosis. Believing the evidence of this conduct, he must not allow himself to be destroyed; he must clad himself in armor. Words, however affectionate, do not count; in fact, they are not to be trusted. The threatening behavior alone is significant. This means that he becomes rebellious or sullen, in any event inimical; or he must hide these reactions beneath an exemplary appearance. Accompanying this securing but unhappy activity is continuous anxiety. Perhaps the effort is not necessary. Perhaps, in discounting the words of affection, he is losing a pearl of great price. Nevertheless in day-by-day life there seems to be no choice. He must dedicate his energy to self-protection against the acts of others. And so, little by little, the defense mechanisms are initiated and strengthened. Character distortions ensue, with the constant element of anxiety. This arises from the hope, all evidence to the contrary, that these distortions, if essential at all, are only for the moment; that he may be incorrect in his judgment of his parents' actions; and that he will soon awake from the nightmare of immediate experience to find the familial environment happy and cherishing. Deep within himself is the refusal to believe what seems self-evident.

The determination to act in accordance with experiential fact, whether word or behavior, yet hoping against hope that this is an unnecessary decision, that the threatening "fact" is untrue: this is the basis of anxiety.

The protections against behavior which the child has felt to be factual threaten to weaken as he leaves his family circle and is confronted by personalities who seem to be essentially different in action from the significant persons of his first years. This tendency is in keeping with his constant hope that his parents, no matter how unloving their conduct, were the fond parents whom he needed. Anxiety continues to function, however, and, as formerly, is based on emotional confusion. Perhaps at last the erected defense, although seeming in childhood to be necessary, is now unnecessary and can be discarded. In his contemporary life it seems to be of no avail. And yet he worries for fear he may be deceiving himself. This is a repetition of the childhood paradox. Whether he attempts a new adjustment or clings to his former method of defense, anxiety pervades him. It appears to be impossible to make any decision in feelings or behavior, in reaction to his surroundings. He is caught in complete helplessness, in confused impotence. All he can feel is anxiety, no matter which way he turns. Whom can he trust? In what act, in what word can he have confidence? At this point he is forced to ask for aid. Someone else must tell him what to do, must make his decisions for him; for he is helpless.

This is the condition, in varying degrees, of all neurotic persons. They are still longing for loving parents; yet they are almost certain, from their childhood experience, that no one will ever value them for themselves. They have finally come to believe that they did not and do not deserve loving care. The records of psychotherapists give proof of the endless attempts of the child to withstand such disillusions. These attempts are fraught with anxiety—not with the fear of an inability to survive but with anxious helplessness in the face of confusion. Hence we find the adult patient longing with anxious hunger, anxiously phantasying in compensation and yet, in self-protection, insisting upon a repetition of his old misfortunes. He cannot but believe them to be again probable. He does not dare to accept them as illusions, without realistic basis, in his present relation with the therapist.

As his trust in the therapist gradually grows stronger, it is certain to be accompanied by an even greater anxiety; for it still seems possible that this trust, which he longs to exercise, may be misplaced. Yet as the months of treatment pass, he recognizes that at last he has found a friend whose wish is for his health and happiness. The relationship gives increasing evidence of fulfilling his lifelong hope that his neurotic protection was in reality a temporary expedient of childhood.

This final conflict is the most acute of all the many encountered in psychotherapeutic treatment. The patient, even now, is confronting the earliest problem of his infancy. He is, however, at last facing it consciously and with determination. He is no longer a helpless infant but a maturing adult; his neurotic symptoms and character distortions have been gradually and painfully conquered; he has won the venture of friendship. He is no longer dependent on unloving and insincere companions; but, having won confidence in his judgment, he determines to choose those whose words and behavior can be trusted. He makes himself responsible for his failure or success. Anxiety now has no place in phantasy or in actuality. It can at last be discarded.

Neurotic worry or anxiety, the product of the self-preservative instinct in face of emotional confusion, maintains its existence as an aura surrounding life. Its chief basis is the all-pervasive dread that the neurotic structure, initiated temporarily in childhood as a self-protection, is in reality an essential and permanent disguise in all human relations. This would mean the worthlessness of one's nature; the denial of life's significance; and the casting away of all joy.

Chapter 7

DEPRESSION

The existence both of manic-depressive psychosis and of neurotic illnesses in which the sufferer experiences alternating moods of heightened elation and extreme melancholy suggests that these moods may be persistent accompaniments of each other. Often at times of elation we fully expect to fall from the heights; that has been our unvarying experience. In depression, however, we do not have any such belief in a sudden and welcome change of emotional weather. In this latter case, when the euphoric phase is apparently absent, it may nevertheless be present unconsciously. This would seem to indicate that the state of depression precedes that of elation and therefore actually takes precedence, is the basic condition; and that elation, whether conscious or unconscious, is in all probability a reaction to depression.

Why should elation succeed depression, and vice versa? There must be a purposeful basis for this progression. I suggest that the euphoric condition is an unconscious therapeutic attempt by the total organism. As a fever is an endeavor by the organism to rid itself of destructive infection, to defeat a hostile external attack, so euphoria is a feverish endeavor to defeat an emotional state of self-destruction, of despair, induced by circumstances external to the sufferer.

It is well known that depression concentrates, in its singleness and its seeming simplicity, manifold wishes and impulses of which its possessor is unaware. It symbolizes impotence, defeat, helplessness, self-devaluation, and self-destruction. It simultaneously expresses a demand for sympathy, at the very least for attention. And it also expresses a passionate but indirect aggression, revenge, and malign counterattack. Depression could be thus paraphrased, "You do not love me, you do not value me, you are annihilating me. Very well! I will be what you demand. I will play myself false and in so doing I will show you what a mess you have made of me. Then you will be sorry. By this mess that I let you make of me, by my self-betrayal, I will shame you and force you to eat your words, to repent, and to take care of me."

This is a vicious circle, like all neuroses and psychoses. The sufferer, in submitting to external power, is in partnership with his own defeat; he is now guilty toward himself. Self-destruction becomes an essential program for him, not only as an attempt to cancel his guilt by self-punishment but mainly as proof of the cruelty of those in power. He may indeed succeed in arousing their attentive concern. But this is a poor substitute for the loving care which is necessary for growth. This need for love he forces himself to disregard, he pretends that it is unessential. Yet it constitutes the one and only milieu which he must have for happy existence. So again by his own admission he finds himself unloved, unvalued, stultified—and must recommence the cycle. Nothing has been achieved except by indirection. This is indeed a self-betrayal. Only guilty despair can result.

Because depression is indirect in its destructive expression toward external forces, in reaction to the invasion of these forces, it is unnatural. It can itself be called a foreign substance, like a malignant growth which has no healthy place or healthy purpose in the organism. The extraordinary power of resistance in living organisms is, however, at war with all foreign bacilli, all foreign invasion. This power ceaselessly carries on a struggle for self-preservation. Therefore the constant insistence on continuing life must find a weapon, some natural force to conquer the depression. The self-evident force is an emotional state that is the very opposite of depression, that in its nature opposes it: this is euphoria.

The state of elation denies all validity in despair. In its feverish tension it insists on the happiness, the exultation, the power of its possessor. It denies the power of those in the external environment. It denies its owner's helplessness; it attempts to prove his happiness and success; it insists upon his value and upon his ability to exist independently of others.

Both states are built on self-deception, and this is the fly in the ointment. In depression, the sufferer persuades himself that he was forced by external circumstances to repudiate his intrinsic nature. In euphoria, he persuades himself that he never actually renounced this essential element. Both are untrue. He did, in the face of a powerful environment, but of his own choice, yield his very essence. Because he is unable to admit this truth he must constantly swing from one extreme of untruth to the other, from the depth of depression to the height of elation.

Psychotherapy has, as one of its many essential tasks, the opportunity to correct the falsehood in both the depressive and the euphoric states. How to assist the patient to recognize these self-deceptions is the problem. Rational interpretations are not sufficient, for the patient cannot accept them. He has unconsciously dedicated his emotional life to these conflicting issues. If he now admits his past guilty behavior toward himself and toward those in power over him, his tendency is to find refuge in the self-deception of euphoria. If he admits the false elements in his euphoric mood, he is plunged into despair. What is the therapist's opening wedge?

These alternating moods, whether succeeding each other or expressed singly, entirely engulf the sufferer. Differing from such neurotic or psychotic symptoms as bodily ills, phobias, obsessions, or compulsions, they are not isolated moments of pain or discomfort or fear, not isolated thoughts or acts. They are instead complete, and often constant, emotional conditions which in themselves may initiate any of the more specific symptoms. It would therefore seem that the most effective therapy would be to deal with the absorbing mood *in toto*, rather than to try to break it down into its detailed forms of expression and then attempt to dispel the mood by dispelling the symptoms. If this thesis is correct, which of these destructive states is of primary importance for the therapeutic attack? And what is the best method of attack?

Exaggerated expression of emotions can be eased by assisting the patient to develop a greater sense of reality, by replacing the element of exaggeration with a beneficial and real substitute. But emotions which are false in themselves, as are euphoria and depression, must be totally renounced in favor of true emotions, those appropriate to a given person in given instances or experiences, that are appropriately aroused by given stimuli. Inappropriateness cannot be outlawed by reason. It must be fully sensed, emotionally experienced. To do this the patient cannot afford to alleviate his moods by opposing depression or euphoria with the other, as was his previous custom. This would be to alternate two inappropriate emotions, never quite giving in to either, and therefore never sensing the complete falsity of either. He must instead be willing to give up this incessant battle and to yield the victory to one of the adversaries. Armed with confidence in the therapist, he must make this decision as a constructive act, with his own benefit in view.

To which of these two moods shall he grant victory? There is no doubt that elation is more welcome than depression. Elation, however, cannot be visualized as an archenemy. Depression is inevitably and intrinsically this enemy in his most threatening form. The facts, therefore, in their very nature, present no choice at all. It is the depressed state that, in the yielding to its intensity, must be used to fight itself, to induce its self-destruction, to eat itself up. The chief characteristic of this emotion is destruction: self-destruction and the indirect destruction of others. It may be that this very characteristic makes it possible for depression to destroy also itself; to consume itself; to reduce the emotional condition of the victim to a comparative blank, to a state of receptivity.

Entrance can then be allowed to emotions that are appropriate, true to the patient's nature. Elation can no longer fill the bill, for it, too, is exaggerated and false. Weakened by the experience of yielding to depression, the sufferer cannot force himself to the old therapeutic attempt of elation. He can but devote himself to the natural process of recuperation. As in physical illness, he must wait for nature to take its course, in faith that health will result.

The therapist, cooperating with the patient in his choice of instrument and method of attack, must allow him the privilege of indulging himself in the depressive condition. The patient's increasing emotional strength, in the course of therapy, eventually permits this indulgence to its full degree without self-destructive danger. This is possible because the patient's trust in his therapist has been firmly established. The therapist is not the powerful and self-willed person whom he had confronted in his childhood. He recognizes that the therapist is standing by him as he sinks into hopelessness. This means that he is essentially *not* hopeless; he has the hope that by yielding to his original pattern of despair he may gain insight. He may learn from this bitter re-experiencing why he did in truth renounce his integrity in face of cruel opposition.

Needless to say this submitting to deep depression cannot be a single experience, it must be the result of increasingly frequent attempts to succumb to such an emotional condition. The patient may at first, and often, suspect the therapist's aim; but with growing trust and insight, he recognizes that together they are pursuing a healthful program—liberation from his neurotic cycle. The patient's eventual willingness to give himself up to his extreme sense of despair may be compared to the willingness of a surgical patient to submit to anesthesia. He believes that he will awake to find himself on the new road to health.

As the patient voluntarily allows this depression to have its way with him, he is upheld in a new belief that he will find the truth about himself. It will no longer be possible for him to deceive himself, for he is certain that at last, and at least in the eyes of his therapist, he is of essential value. This confidence enables him to relax into the experience of his childhood. What, as he reviews it with adult eyes, did actually happen?

Through his new attitude he sees by way of his depression the factual experiences of his infancy: the fears, the disillusions, the self-protections. He recognizes the disappointments, the anger, the impotence in expressing this anger, the need to be acknowledged in his own right. Although he also recognizes the disastrous mistakes made by the significant persons in his childhood, he accepts his submission to their power as a self-betrayal and finds in himself a need, until now unconscious, to forgive them and a wish to be reconciled with them.

From this re-experiencing of himself as a child, he can understand and sympathize with himself in his euphoric refusal to admit the condition of being unloved and his euphoric insistence that all is for the best in this best of all possible worlds. He now appreciates his self-preservative attempts in both depressive and manic moods. He comes to acknowledge that his obsession with these extreme and opposite states also constitutes an insistence that he be delivered from this unwholesome concern with the cruelty of others.

There results a realization that he must in fact deliver, must save himself. No euphoric mood will accomplish this self-rescue, for it, like his depression, is false. He must come down to earth and see himself as an individual like all others, struggling to find his own worth, his particular value as a human being—and, as such, his value to himself and to mankind.

This willingness to *relax* into depression, in its extreme expression and in company with the therapist, allows an insight never before realized. The chance to review safely his infantile experience of rejection breaks the vicious circle of his neurosis. He has learned to accept his therapist's recognition of him, and hence to acknowledge to himself his own value. There is no longer a need for extreme depression, a self-betrayal in indirect vengeance. And there is no longer a need for false exultation.

Chapter 8

HOSTILE PROTEST AND REVENGE

That the conflict between parent and child should continue in our culture, which stresses intelligence, is a problem that not only psychologists but sociologists must solve. On the psychotherapists' shoulders lies the immediate burden of therapy when the result of this conflict is emotional ill-health. How can the child be assisted in preserving his selfhood in the face of his parents' insistent principles of behavior and morality, and in the face of their overwhelming potency? How can he guard his own nature intact in the face of his need for the loving protection of these very parents? Or, as an adult, how can he regain his sense of self-determination, how can he visualize and free himself from his parents, the often well-meaning but blind figures of his innocent childhood? If he resurrects his actual infantile experience at the mercy of these powerful forces, how can he deal in the present with such an undigested experience? How can he dispel the ghostlike influence of the significant figures of the past?

The answer to these fundamental questions lies in the bringing into the neurotic patient's consciousness of the accurate memory, from the child's point of view, of his struggle with his parents; in an acknowledgment that the need for loving care seduced him as a child, necessitating the rejection of his own demands of growth, and the succumbing to the demands of the environment; and in a re-evaluation, according to his contemporary standards, of his total situation in childhood. The answer also lies in his recognition that the frustration of his inherent need to live lovingly resulted in repressing and forgetting the fact that his submission was accompanied by an anger at giving way, and by a consequent unconscious dedication of his life to proving the dominating blindness or cruelty of his parents. "If you demand this of me, I must yield to you; but I hate you for it and will show you up!"

This angry protest or revenge lies buried deep beneath the childhood attempt to adjust with loving, or even slightly rebellious, reaction to the parents' insistent molding of his personality.

Few patients will at the outset of treatment admit their hatred of their parents. Even when they do, the admission often represents a surface rebellion, which hides their early submission to those powerful forces. Yet in the lives of all neurotic patients, in their behavior toward others, they clearly show a vengeful spirit. This spirit underlies a paranoid suspicion of their fellow men, a schizoid repression of emotions, a catatonic refusal of mobility, an obsessive emphasis on intellectuality; it underlies phobic and hysterical symptoms; and it underlies varied maladjustments in their personal relations with contemporary society. Each such patient hides from himself and from others his unwitting choice of a life of hostile revenge.

In infancy his individual quality led his parents to see him as a stranger—often unwanted, disliked, or rejected. With the development of his idiosyncratic temperament, his parents expose him to experiences of being molded, and of consequent frustration. In reaction, he must unconsciously decide upon the pursuit of his life's path. If he is of strong and courageous constitution he may determine against all odds to assert his individuality. In this case—and such cases are all too few—he remains comparatively healthy. Or he may begin to fix his gaze upon the external powers which force their imitation upon him. He now loses his own likeness and accommodates himself to the likeness of others. Inherent in this latter unconscious decision is the inhibition of his nature and the incipience of the motive of revenge.

We now see in this acquired personality a deep falsity and, in consequence, an unconscious anger at being forced into such falsehood. This anger is a self-assertive sign, for it is the only true and typical function which remains of his own nature. It at least announces: "I am still I. If I must die, I die fighting!"

Therapeutic assistance must face this total situation. It must elicit in the patient conscious recognition of this hypocrisy and the resulting hostility. In what form does he reveal his falsity and its accompanying motive of revenge?

As examples, I give the following accounts of the early experience of two patients.

One patient, thirty-five years of age, a priest, had unwittingly given over his fate into the hands of his parents.

The youngest of four children, he remained for many years the blond and curly-haired favorite of his mother. She beguiled him, by her physical attentions and by her anxious protectiveness, into assuming a passive role. He was not allowed the companionship of his older brother, which would have led him into boyish dangers, nor that of his father, which would have taught him to become an active farmer's son. His only childhood companion was his mother, a stern churchwoman, a firm believer in original sin, and fearful of worldly ways. Her baby was from birth dedicated by her to the church.

He remembers his longing to play with the boys of his own age, his wish to take part in the farm activities, his resentment at religious rituals, both at home and at church. He remembers also his pleasure in his mother's constant attentiveness, her bribery and corruption. She bathed him until his twelfth year. Often he slept in her bed. His adolescent phantasy took this form: If his mother would pursue her physical care of him in recognition of his growing sexual impulses, she would then teach him to attain his manhood. Then he could take his rightful place with his brother and father, both of whom had always neglected him and despised him as a "sissy." It was in these years of his early teens that his mother, sensing his sexual demands, reproved and rejected him. This meant for him the frustration, the denial, of his manhood and the final loss of brother and of both parents. He belonged to no one. The outside world could have no use for this untutored boy. The members of his family despised him.

In dismay he turned to the only source of security, the church. Here he could redeem himself in his mother's eyes and could take an esteemed place with his brother and father, both of whom were active church members. He could indeed attain a superiority to these men of the family, to most men, by becoming a famous preacher. This would prove his worth and give him, in his superior eminence, the opportunity simultaneously to revenge himself upon his mother for her rejection and upon his father and brother for their neglect and for their refusal to rescue him from his mother.

To become a priest was an easy goal, for he possessed an excellent mind, an appealing presence, and an interest in social betterment. He won a certain success, but this was increasingly undermined by a spirit of malicious vengeance. He began to delight in accusing his parishioners of their evil doings. Increasingly aware of the danger of this compulsion, he sought therapeutic aid. He could not understand his constant temptation to preach angry sermons; his attitude of spite and contempt toward the women of his congregation; and, during the church services, his frequent hysterical symptoms of compulsive blushing, dizziness, and liability to fainting spells.

Under therapy he discovered that his role as priest functioned as a self-bribe, with its financially secure and easy life, with the beauty of the church ritual, with the opportunity for fame. It assured him a respected position among the men and women of the community. It also protected him, in his asceticism, from his sexual impulses, originally disapproved of by his mother in his adolescent years. But, above all, his priestly role allowed him the expression of self-righteous anger and hostility, disguised as "hunger and thirst after righteousness." This early passionate need to revenge himself on his childhood family threatened increasingly to pour itself out in hatred upon his congregation and, in so doing, to undo his dedication to the church and to bring about the destruction of his sanity.

A second patient, an accountant by profession, forty years old, complained in his first interview that he could never keep a job for more than a few years. In each position he began at the bottom, learning the business from the beginning. He then easily reached a position of importance and responsibility. Anxiety then overcame him; he found it impossible to delegate responsibility; he felt himself compelled to attend to each simple duty; he found no day long enough for the carrying out of this compulsion; he began to procrastinate, to overlook essential tasks; he began to fear the displeasure of his superiors. In the end he forced himself to resign his position, but left the company with excellent references and to the regret of his co-workers. This cycle repeated itself ad infinitum. He finally became convinced that he was moved by some powerful unconscious determinant, and needed psychotherapeutic help.

He had been trained from his earliest years to "please others"—

to forget himself, to be as others wished, but especially "to please." Although of native intelligence and curiosity, his capacity for interests remained undifferentiated; he could not specify any particular concern. "I am interested in everything. I've never known anything that did not interest me." His curiosity, however, remained entirely unexplored. His only wish expressed itself as a determination to use his keen sensitivity to learn what others wished of him, and to succeed in assuming all responsibilities that might be thrust upon him.

The physical symptom of duodenal ulcers gave hint of a childhood oral frustration. This hint was eventually substantiated when he spoke of the extreme poverty of his early years, of the large number of stepbrothers and stepsisters from his father's first marriage and again in later years from his mother's second marriage. Another important substantiation lay in the story of his father's death, when he himself was a child of five. He remembers the scene with his sorrowing mother and grown stepbrothers around the deathbed. His mother was then eight months pregnant. He remembers the solemn words of his dying father: "Now, son, you will be the man of the family. You must care for and support your mother!" "And I always have," continued the patient. "From the time I was eight years old, caddying at the golf links, I have given my mother one third of what I earned. One third went to her for my board, one third to her for herself, and I kept the other third."

He remembers no emotional reaction to his father's death: no sorrow, no pity for his mother or for himself, no anxiety, no rebellion at the unsuitable and unfair behest of his father. He loved both parents and was kindly treated by them. He was happy at his mother's second marriage two years later. He loved his stepfather and the two new stepbrothers, who, again, were much older than himself. Caught between two sets of grown step-siblings, who were devotedly cared for by his mother and were able, but unwilling, to assist in her support, this child assumed without conscious resentment the partial support of his mother and himself. He was her one and only son. To care for her was his duty, as impressed upon him by his father.

That he accepted this duty with conscious willingness seemed to be due to his devotion to his parents, to the entire family; to the insistent training to please others; and to the emotional fact that at the age of five he was prematurely regarded as a grown man. Deprived of the recognition of his childhood needs for dependence and support (food and shelter), he was forced to repress these yearnings and to replace them with a totally false outlook on life. In one moment he gave up his position as a child and became a substitute father. The adults of his family, especially his mother, became for him his children. No wonder that the digestive tract of this patient, starved for the emotional nourishment of childhood, developed additional mouths by way of ulcers.

He remembers only one occasion of resentment in all his boyhood. Himself the youngest caddy on the links, he resented the long hours of waiting for a client and the dirty stories and words used by the older boys. He forced himself to learn these, in order to please his companions. But he also trained himself to eliminate these words from his vocabulary when at home, in order not to displease his "parents."

It seems almost impossible that such a childhood environment would not have created a conscious rebellion in this patient. That his rebellion was thrust into the unconscious realm was undoubtedly due to his sensitive affection for his kindly "parents" and to their insistence on the expression of his loving-kindness to others, a loving-kindness which was in keeping with his essential nature.

It was, however, inevitable that the lifelong distortion of this natural gift at the hands of others, even though with his own connivance, should initiate unconscious hostility. He could not be consciously angry and vengeful and at the same time be "pleasing." The revenge must therefore assert itself in neurosis. This assertion took form whenever the patient in his later years had proved his capacity for responsibility. At this point he would begin his program of self-sabotage. He felt himself failing in his responsibilities. He feared the consequent displeasure of others. He forced himself to resign his job but kept the respect and good will of those in superior positions. And again he must start at the bottom of the ladder as if a little boy of five. In this symbolic way he cried out for succor and support. He unconsciously called attention to the fact that he was too young to be held responsible for the support of others; that if they insisted on his being grown up, he would show them that they asked too much of him; he would fail them and himself; he would, after raising their hopes, dash them again. His neurosis was thus not only a cry from his heart that he was a starving child in need of nourishment. It was also an attempt to punish all adults, all those in any way superior to him, for not recognizing his need and fulfilling it, and for their unfair and overwhelming demands upon him.

Each neurotic sufferer has developed his particular form of neurosis as a hostile expression of protest and revenge. The parents' power need not have been cruelly used. Indeed, it is more often well intentioned, and even kindly, as in the case of the second patient. But it must have been forceful and dominating. And it must have left no doubt in the child's mind as to the existence of authority in the parental figures. This predicates submission on the child's part. If rebellion is partly conscious, it must be immediately repressed because of the child's need for security and love. This need is corruptible, easily seduced and falsified. A whole system of distorted and false values is then initiated by the hungry child at the hands of those who are physically and emotionally in power.

The dynamics of neurosis can be freed from such distortion and be healthily reintegrated only by the dynamics of therapy. The poison of hatred and vengeance can be distilled away only by the therapy of love. Therefore, the essential element in psychotherapy consists in rendering useless the unconscious attempt of the patient to revenge himself on the overpowering ghosts of the past. Although these attempts have always proved impotent, never having brought the significant figures or their surrogates to their knees, they have continued compulsively, with the hope of eventual success. This hope must, with the therapist's aid, be proved unfounded. It must be exchanged for a new set of value standards. This exchange can only occur with the realization that there is in the therapeutic situation no question of authority, of domination, whether kind or cruel. There is no impingement of standards or values of one co-worker upon the other. There must be, on the contrary, a mutuality of respect and regard, a sharing of responsibilities.

As the neurotic patient yields, in therapy, his useless resentment and revenge against the forceful and destructive figures of the past, he faces a healthy present which requires no submission and a future in which he will retrieve and develop the buried constructive elements of his nature.

PART III. Integral Goals of Psychoanalysis

CHAPTER 9

THE RESTORATION OF PERSONAL INTEGRITY

THERE are certain deterrent character traits inevitably present in all psychoneurotic personalities. Arrogance or self-abasement; emotional deadness, automatism, or hypersensitivity; a degree of blindness to the actual events of reality or a continual misinterpretation of an acute awareness of reality: one of these is always to be found, and in an exaggerated form. They are accompanied by a more or less veiled self-destructive impulse, by a tendency toward indirect vengeance, and by a resulting incapacity to form successful personal relationships; and they are permeated throughout by anxiety and guilt. What is the function of these ever-present injurious characteristics? They have not, we believe, evolved as natural direct expressions of individuality but as necessary steps in adjustment to the demands of the environment. They must therefore have a self-preservative purpose; yet they are called neurotic because to all intents they result in self-destruction, in illness and disability. They can be said to be the better of two evils, for it is better to be maimed than annihilated, better to have ugly scar tissue than an open wound.

The choice has been necessitated by traumatic occurrences in early childhood which wound so suddenly or so recurrently the core of the child's personality that for the moment the growth impulse is stunned. The direct and open channel of growth is damaged and blocked. It must therefore be sealed off and a new channel be quickly opened before the life-stream ceases altogether. Hence scar tissue is formed and a deformity results as a reaction to damage. This replaces the original pure outgrowth from the seed.

As one organ of the body compensates for another that is diseased or destroyed, or a part of the heart compensates for another part that has ceased to function, the new and distorted method of expressing his impulses is an unconscious attempt on the part of the child to compensate for the serious hurt to his essential characteristic nature and its forthright expression. As in the case of the diseased heart, the original balanced equation is put out of kilter; the compensation tends to become exaggerated and overheavy, and results in an organ or personality dissimilar to the original and unhealthy in expression.

It may seem difficult to believe that the central core of a child's nature can be harmed to such an extent. One can only predicate that, as the study of neuroses has proved the existence of this possibility, disastrous experiences in childhood must often be more potent than the ability of the child to withstand them. On the other hand, the growth impulse is itself proved to be indomitable by the very fact that the child does not succumb completely to the traumatic occurrences but fights for life even at the expense of developing a neurotic personality, indeed by way of his neurosis.

If the neurosis is a temporarily effective, although ultimately destructive, compensation, what becomes of the damaged and impotent constitutional nature which it displaces? Does it slough off and disappear? Or does it maintain a stifled existence cut off from and out of touch with the new distorted image of itself? It is possible that even in the most severe psychoses the essential integrity of the sufferer is not completely destroyed. Certainly in psychoneurotics it is within reach and can be tapped and released. Therefore, to render powerless and to dissipate the harmful compensating adjustment is only half the task of psychotherapy. There must accompany this the even more important task of reviving and nourishing, strengthening and maturing the original nature of the neurotic patient.

If one studies closely the progress of psychoanalytic treatment, one can see on the part of both patient and analyst these two undertakings constantly and simultaneously in process. The patient in seeking aid gives immediate evidence that the fight for the persistence of his inherent nature has not ceased but is still in action. His need and endeavor to trust the analyst betoken the same effort. These beneficial elements are, however, accompanied through much of the therapeutic treatment, and are frequently almost overshadowed, by the characteristic habits of action and thought which spring from his neurotic attempt to appease his environment.

Since the healthy impulse is weak and tentative, the first aim of the therapist is to bring to the patient's consciousness a greater realization of his worth, before beginning the breakdown of the neurotic edifice. This is possible because, in making the acquaintance of his patient, he must have sensed the hidden capacity and potentiality, the inherent value, of his character. The slight encouragement is then closely followed by a careful and tactful examination of the defense mechanisms; at first the more superficial, gradually the more entrenched. A small degree of anxious hostility is inevitably awakened in the patient by this seeming criticism. It is, however, combined with an increase of confidence in the analyst's perspicacity and helpful interest. Such slight signs of emotional conflict at the beginning of treatment represent the basic conflict of the neurosis, which constantly repeats itself in varied guises and circumstances, and with growing vigor. The increasingly vigorous struggle signifies a more powerful attempt by the integral core of the patient's personality to break through the imprisoning bars of the neurotic protection. In this struggle the analyst seems to the patient to take sides alternately with each of the opposed forces, seems constantly to symbolize the stronger side, forcing the patient to strengthen the weaker in order to win the battle. The patient's sense of reality, however, can be counted upon to function more effectively as his true nature gets the upper hand. It gradually dawns upon him that the analyst is in reality always on the side of his heretofore imprisoned self and that the appeasing neurotic mechanisms are proved to be unnecessary in this mutual relationship. He recognizes that he has unconsciously forced the analyst into illusory roles and that in giving up these illusions he has finally succeeded in overthrowing the neurotic organization. No longer caught in the vicious circle of his neurosis, he can now function as an independent entity. The adventure of developing his gifts and temperament lies before him.

Hence we see that when the patient is given an appropriate environment in the form of a technically skilled and sympathetic analyst, the two essential therapeutic trends inevitably begin to function. This is exemplified in the case of a young man whose severe depressions drove him to seek psychoanalytic assistance. His rather feeble wish to recover his emotional health could only be expressed by him as a doubtful hope that his treatment would not result in establishing in him the belief, which his parents had urgently preached, that to be "natural" was evil and destructive, and would not force him to give up his "natural" impulses. He had to admit that he was barely aware of these latter, and yet he clung to them. In other words, in coming to an analyst he was searching for a parent who would value him for himself, who would tenderly help him to develop as an individual. He feared, however, that even psychoanalysis, his last resort, held no hope of success in this search.

The distorted and twisted compensation can be recognized in this expression of his hopes and fears. It continued to be voiced through the early part of his treatment in a stilted and intellectualized language and in words so subdued as to be almost indistinguishable. His actions, thoughts, and feelings were stiff and awkward. He seemed to be in a constant emotional stupor. When some expression of his more positive wishes slipped through a crevice in his protective armor, he would anxiously apologize and would be sunk in depression at the next analytic appointment. From his stolen and guilty enjoyment in writing witty light verse, in indulgence in drawing lessons, in the emotional rather than intellectual delight in music, in his wish to escape from his family over frequent week-ends, and in his diffident but charming smile, the lively free nature of his inherent personality was seen—in high contrast to his usual automatic behavior and somber, dubious, and unhappy attitudes.

It was necessary at the beginning of the treatment of this patient to educe and stress his tentative and innocent desires, constantly urging him to tell me sincerely of his true wishes and feelings instead of the beliefs and standards which he for the moment considered his own, but seemed often to be expressing in quotes. He would preach long and earnest sermons on moral questions. When I inquired whether he really believed these pronouncements, he was at first startled but would then settle down to an honest examination of his own principles, admitting that he had been imitating his father, a minister of the church, and that he believed in reality that most of his father's ideas were nonsense. It proved beneficial to tell him of my ideas of the moral issues presented by him and also to lend him encouragement by expressing my own feeling that even as a little boy he was more intuitive and wiser in his understanding of human actions and relationships than either of his parents. As a result of the slight strengthening of his inner integrity at this early point in the analysis, he became more relaxed, less emotionally catatonic, and more free to observe and take stock of his pompous protections.

To woo the natural self in the early stages of treatment into slight expression, without frightening it back into seclusion and thereby increasing the need to strengthen the protections, draws upon the analyst's skill. This is achieved in all analyses by the balanced procedure of tactfully drawing attention to the evidences of the patient's true nature, which he has so diffidently shown, and also to his various defensive methods of action and thought. Bringing these opposed impulses to conscious attention and out into the light, without criticism or blame but simply as facts, enables the patient and analyst to study together the possible reasons for defense, with the hope that any useless defense may be discarded. Needless to say, such an action, even though often recognized by the patient as desirable, cannot at this time be done by will power. It occurs involuntarily and inevitably as the patient grows in confidence, both in himself and in his analyst, and hence as the need for defense in this particular relationship lessens.

As the analysis proceeds, the natural impulses of the patient are more spontaneously expressed. The protective measures also are proportionately more active. The increased vigor of his innate wishes and demands forces him unconsciously to strengthen his past methods of controlling them. The moment comes, however, when he catches a glimpse of himself, "the indestructible me," as standing apart from the shackles of the threatening past, naked and unafraid. At this time dreams of nakedness often change in emphasis and significance from a fear of being seen naked, or a rebellious insistence on being naked among others fully clothed, to an enjoyment of nakedness in appropriate surroundings. Yet this first glimpse of his true self seems to disappear like a mirage as the patient stretches out his hand to seize it. Only after constant repetitive and successful struggles with his fears and anxieties does it again return; each reappearance tends to remain a little longer and to seem more solid and genuine, more desirable. Now at last he sees and feels and is reacquainted with a mirrored reflection of himself as someone he not only longs to be but believes he can be. The goal of treatment is for the first time in sight. There is something tangible and real to work for. At last he is able to struggle consciously and voluntarily to rid himself of his protective chains. As his regained natural strength comes fully to his assistance, they seem to fall away as if by magic.

An example of this new awareness of strength is shown in the case of a young man suffering from alcoholism. Underlying this symptom were semiconscious but overpowering feelings of shame and worthlessness. As these feelings came to consciousness and he allowed himself to be immersed in them, setting aside his defenses against them, a growing sense of his power to stand such emotional turmoil began to banish the old fear of powerlessness against it. One day he said to me: "Yesterday afternoon I thought that I would have a drink. But I suddenly knew that I was only using that as a means to relieve my horrible feelings, to change them—as it always does. So I lay thinking it out and, *for the first time in my life* that I can ever remember, I did not do it. I got up instead and cleaned out the garage. It's the first time I've ever had strength to resist weakness, and I was very surprised to find that I had not given way to it. Really surprised." The next day he said: "It would be too bad not to overcome the liquor business on my own, before some ailment like ulcers or cirrhosis of the liver sets in. Then I'd *have* to quit it, and would never have the feeling I'd done it with my own strength and courage. I would be really very sorry if something, an outside factor, came along and made me stop, because it would rob me of a victory.

As I unearth more of the stagnant swamp inside of me, I believe I just will automatically not feel the need of liquor. Only lately have I had the idea that I would be pleased and *proud* of myself —for *myself* alone, not for you, though I'd enjoy your awareness and pleasure in my conquest. And with that idea has come a haunting anxiety that some physical ailment may develop that will deprive me of a victory I *must* have. Never before has it appeared in that way. The experience of yesterday came suddenly, with no preliminary build-up of strength or resolution. Well, a struggle it is, and no doubt it will go on being one; but I know perfectly well that I must stick it out and win out. There really isn't any other alternative that I care to accept in my heart."

From these remarks one immediately senses a greatly strengthened integrity of purpose in this patient, as well as a clear understanding of himself. The fact that he continued to slip back one step with each two forward was proof of his growing strength rather than a discouragement. The main problem throughout psychoanalytic treatment is the nourishing and encouraging of the patient's power to grow in his own right. This can be a permanent accomplishment only if carried out in direct challenge to the facts of his emotional reality. In the case of this young man, only by succumbing to the feelings of extreme loneliness and unlovableness and by learning of his ability to endure these feelings, hitherto repressed, did he sense his native strength and add to it. Without this intense conflict and its frequent setback the tools which he already possessed and now needed for a constructive life would not have been sharpened. Yet only thus could he search for his true personality.

One aim of psychoanalytic therapy is that of freeing the neurotic patient from the protections which his childhood environment has forced upon him. The other and more constructive aim is the search for the patient's true personality. The terms "core of personality," "inner self," "true nature," and "personal integrity" are extremely elusive to define. Yet every human being knows in his heart what they represent; for he is chiefly concerned throughout his life, consciously or unconsciously, in preserving his integrity and in allowing his nature to come to expression. Indeed the neurosis which he may develop originates for the very purpose of preserving his integrity. One's self, whether it be represented by one's body or one's spirit, must be guarded at all cost. It must be saved even though it be lost in the process. Here we see the paradox represented in all neuroses and psychoses. It is the chief task of the psychotherapist to help his patient to surmount this paradox by opening wide the path to the free expression of man's inherent moral nature.

Chapter 10

SELF-CONTROL

Psychoanalytic research has come increasingly to recognize that all neuroses are basically character disorders; that any symptom may appear or disappear during analytic treatment; and that, until the fundamental nature of the patient is discovered and rescued from emotional conflict, we have no lasting freedom from any neurotic symptom. Psychoanalytic therapy, therefore, is at present evolving from its earlier concentration on emotional catharsis. In its most recent form its chief concern is with the possibility of character development.

Such qualities as loving-kindness or hatred, nonpossessiveness or jealousy and envy, amiable or ill-natured humor, generosity or selfishness, cruelty or submission to cruelty, although always of interest as human traits, take on a new significance when we consider their origin in childhood, how they developed, and how they became exaggerated; when we consider how they are at present manifested, in what way they are directly or indirectly used, what part they play in personal relations, and whether they increase or decrease the productivity and happiness of their possessors. Could we choose for ourselves among these many qualities and their expression, there would be no doubt of our choice. That we often tend unconsciously to choose the more deleterious is the result of character deformation—and it is this deformity that psychotherapy seeks to correct.

The first effort of the corrective process should be to recognize the full scope of the deformity, its origin and nature, its development, and its compensating qualities. How in functioning does it bribe and corrupt its possessor, so that it may maintain its existence? What strange rationalizations does it use? When the patient has discovered the deforming characteristics, how may he be enlightened so that he sees their true nature, their present uselessness and parasitic quality; so that he may determine to rid himself of such an incubus? When he so determines, how can he be assisted to develop his new strength so that there may be no need for further neurotic weapons in the struggle for a healthy and constructive existence? These questions suggest, in the large, what occurs in the many months of analytic therapy.

In the course of treatment a point is always reached at which the patient comes to recognize to the full his neurotic misconstructions and wishes to cast them aside—is determined so to do. He is also eager to develop his new-found capacities, to exercise and mature his inherent personality. It is at this period in treatment that the factor of self-control comes into beneficent play.

The puritanical conception of the term "self-control" stresses the word "control." Psychoanalytic emphasis is on the word "self"; for without knowledge of our self, we have nothing to control. Our forebears dogmatically preached the use of "will power" because of their anxious fear of the unknown in themselves. This unknown consisted chiefly in the life of the emotions and its expression. We now know that overweaning anxiety may in itself be one primary cause of evil. It stimulates incomparably the forces of hostile self-defense and revenge. And it is these two forces which lead inevitably to neurotic structures.

The "self-control" of our immediate ancestors, therefore, was a manifestation of neurosis, both in cause and effect. Self-knowledge, on the other hand, eradicates anxiety, dispersing neurosis. It brings the opportunity to choose between alternative actions. It results in the freeing of creative power. This power must be used productively, and it must be channeled. It must therefore be controlled.

The impulse for self-expression is born in us. Like all impulses it is at first diffuse and experimental. To be of greatest service it should gradually become specific. This comes as the result of healthy and happy contact with our environment. The harmful experiences of infancy, on the contrary, have produced false limitations, those imposed on us from without. Through the beneficial experience of psychotherapy these should be replaced by self-limitations. To control ourselves is as fundamental a need as self-expression. Both of these needs and their satisfactions must be realized in any successful psychoanalytic treatment.

It is essential to examine closely the nature and function of self-control as it develops during psychoanalytic therapy. It is a control, not of the possession and realization of emotions themselves, but of the choice of which emotions to express and of their method of expression: in other words, of behavior. Here again is seen a contrast to the puritanical preachments. In these there was recognized no distinction between feelings and their expression. We were commanded to destroy in us the feelings of hatred and to entertain only the feelings of love. We were in the same breath given commands in regard to our actions —we were told not to kill, nor to steal, nor to commit adultery— and we were given the Golden Rule. Emotions and the actions based on these emotions were grouped in one confused category. In reality they form two categories which cannot be compared, for they are generically dissimilar. Feelings are the motive power of behavior. Behavior results from the stimulation of feelings. The possession and strength of feelings are beyond control; they exist involuntarily as facts and form the basis of our nature. They can in childhood be repressed below our consciousness; but they carry on their existence in the unconscious realm as long as there is life in us. They cannot be destroyed. When we hold them in our consciousness, however, we have the choice and power to act or to refuse to act upon them. It is with this power that self-control must deal.

The emotional life of the patient undergoing psychoanalytic treatment is the basic material of whatever insight is gained. He resurrects those feelings which have been repressed. He examines them, together with those already conscious, in the light of their appropriateness to given stimuli, both of the past and of the present. He gradually allows himself to experience their full strength and learns to sense the power of passion, according to his nature. But when he investigates his customary reactions to these emotions in thought and behavior, he crosses over into a different psychological realm, that of expression.

It is generally feared that once an emotion is in force it must be acted upon. This is an erroneous conception; for there is no necessary link connecting such cause and effect. There is no such *quid pro quo*. It is this falsehood from which all neurotics suffer. Their will power has been worn down in the inevitably unsuccessful attempt to deny the existence in themselves of threatening emotions. In this battle all feelings, both desirable and undesirable, tend to be suppressed, to be negated; for in order to put out of existence the frightening feelings, the actual source of all feeling would need to be quenched. This attempt results in the weakening of emotional capacity, in the possible death of the human being as a consciously feeling person and leads to the full flowering of neurosis.

As a result of the increasing knowledge of our emotional life, psychoanalytic treatment endeavors to give rebirth to the emotional dayspring in each patient. Every feeling is invited. But until the nature and strength of these feelings are recognized, behavior in reaction to them is discouraged. The successful outcome of this difficult struggle is made possible by the fact that all feelings can be and should be expressed *in words* in the analytic relationship, directed toward the analyst in person. The courage to do this rests upon the patient's increasing trust in the wish and capacity of the analyst to assist him to health. The discovery that verbal expression of any and all emotions is a harmless experience, and does not result in rejection or destruction, marks an important step in progress. The patient grows increasingly able to compete with the anxiety that has heretofore accompanied all sensing of strong feeling. This anxiety was due in great part to his belief that such feeling must result in action. He becomes able little by little to estimate the probable outcome of any action so stimulated, and his sense of reality improves. He recognizes himself as a person of emotional potency. He sees others in their emotional strength.

Health makes its first appearance when the patient, no matter how petty the circumstance, can sense his true emotions, those which are appropriate for him in a given instance, and can decide whether or not to act upon them. He has looked into the past and has seen his former temptation to react to emotional stimuli in a way which was dangerous for himself and for others. He can now choose his path of behavior. This necessitates a revived will power and true control.

At the outset of therapy the neurotic patient complains of his lack of self-control. He suffers from physical ailments for which no organic cause can be found; he is possessed by phobias; he is overridden with anxiety; he finds himself irresistibly compelled to act against his reason; his obsessive phantasies interfere with the pursuit of his life; he suffers from uncontrollable jealousy or anger; he is so driven to destroy himself or others that he perforce leads the life of a hermit. Each complaint has the constant element of an inability to control some factor in himself, of being at odds with himself. There is seldom a patient who does not say in his first interview: "I know that I should be able to control myself but I don't seem able to." This is an instance of the prevailing fact that whatever the patient says is true, if only it can be fully understood. Although he may fancy that it is the old-fashioned "will power" in which he is lacking, the analyst knows that it is self-knowledge which he lacks. Hence the analyst's primary aim is the fulfillment of this need.

Because of the distorted ideas and values which neurotic persons have in regard to themselves and the world around them, each attempt to use "will power" is based upon an untruth and hence goes astray. Analytic therapy therefore must lead the erring sufferer back to the path of real values. The patient must be enabled to see the facts of his emotional life as they are. If he is obsessed with the desire to help others, he must eventually realize that this may be a desire to have power over others and even to destroy them—and that it is always a cry from his own heart for help. The alcoholic must learn that his use of alcohol is for the purpose of intensifying his emotional confusion so that he need not feel his deeply suppressed guilt and shame. The patient who cannot succeed in loving relationships must recognize that he dislikes and avoids his fellow men because their presence may arouse in him murderous anger, which he inevitably fears. The patient who insists on his worthlessness must be helped to understand that this is an avoidance of responsibility for his actions and to recognize also the falsity of his self-depreciation. In every instance the misconceptions of the neurotic sufferer must be set straight.

It should be apparent how hopeless is any attempt beneficially to "control" a self deluded with false premises. Once these misconstrued ideas, and any action based on them, are correctly judged during the experience of psychotherapeutic treatment, the basic need for self-control has an opportunity for satisfaction. With the acquisition of each facet of insight a new strength is felt. The wish to use this strength is implicit in every human being. The question then arises: How can one for one's happiness acquire and exercise this capability? Here true control enters upon the scene. The former unhealthy trends continue to offer temptation but the newly gained understanding of these trends and their expression gives warning of failure, of inevitable unhappiness. The patient can now consciously visualize the alternatives. He must learn to exercise his choice, he must exercise his will, he must at last use self-control.

This control is now based on self-knowledge and on a new understanding of others, of the laws by which human beings actually function. These he has begun to learn in his relationship with his analyst. If he has formerly been obsessed "to be helpful," he has during treatment tried indirectly to gain power over his analyst under the guise of some form of "helping," only to find that this attempted use of power was for the purpose of acquiring reassurance in the depths of his insecurity. If through his alcoholism he has added to his emotional confusion, in order to avoid the feelings of shame of which he has heretofore been only dimly conscious, he is at last able to admit his shame to his analyst and to sense it thoroughly; and he can discard his alcoholism. If he has protected himself from his angry impulses by a dislike of people in general, he has now discovered that he can safely express his anger toward his analyst; that his anger does not result in his own destruction nor in that of his analyst; and that as a result he can at will discard his angry expressions, be increasingly aware of his loving-kindness, and hence be able to make and keep friends. If he no longer needs to hide in his analyst's eyes behind a false idea of his worthlessness but instead recognizes his value, he can accept responsibility for himself and for his actions. In each of these patients the time comes when he must admit the falsity of his neurotic misconceptions and must decide for himself to abide by the truth. In this decision his happiness lies. Self-control becomes an important instrument in its achievement.

As examples of the birth and growth of self-control I offer two instances. In analytic treatment the wish to control one's self makes its initial appearance almost under a disguise, often negatively expressed and very feeble. This is due to its early severe distortion. Although most parents insist upon control, they insist upon a control which is in accord with their own ideas, ideas which are all too frequently an appeasement of their social surroundings. As a result the child is forced to subdue the impulses which arise from his individual character and to replace these with substitutes which are inappropriate to his nature. In this process he loses contact with his true self and as nearly as possible becomes a mirrored image of his parents as it is impressed upon him; or, as a rebellious reaction, its exact opposite. This indeed implies a certain control—in this instance an unconscious control with self-preservative aim. Because no alternative is permissible this course eventually represents self-destruction rather than growth, neurosis rather than healthy development.

A young professional woman consulted me because of character difficulties. She insisted that her unfortunate marital situation could never be altered but that she hoped to change her character so as to be able to bear her difficulties with greater equanimity. This expression in itself gives evidence of a wish for control over herself and simultaneously of a fear of losing it when confronting her environment. Her first admission to me was that she lied, that she played tricks on others, that she succeeded in making a false impression on everyone she met and was as a result unwarrantably liked and admired. Several months of treatment were spent in the listing and the describing of her "neurotic" attitudes, her emotional weakness, and her hypocrisy. In keeping with her warning, I liked her immediately. She seemed to me sincere and earnest in our work together. From outside sources I heard favorable reports of her professional ability. I read an excellent book which she had written. Yet she seemed a timid person, lacking in spontaneity. Scarcely a day passed without her insistence that she was not as worthwhile as she seemed.

As she traced the story of her life, one fact stood out beyond all others. She had been surrounded as a child by unusually insincere adults, had listened to the bombastic stories of their prowess and heroism, and had been forced by them to play a hypocritical role in order to gain their admiration by imitating their false superiority. By this she was pretending to be other than she was. And yet, even as a child, she had not quite believed the tales they told or the principles of behavior which they expressed. Always there had been in her a wish to find her way through this maze to the truth. This purposeful wish had, however, been engulfed by complete confusion. If she was to be safely accepted by those around her, she could not afford to pursue the truth, as she believed it to be, but must forget what truths she had already proved and must pretend to be as her parents wished her, like themselves. In this hopeless situation of self-betrayal, she set about trying to be a "good child," superior to the other children. This attempt was suffused with a fear of incapacity to live up to the expectations of her parents and with an anxiety that this incapacity might be discovered. And so throughout her life she swung from exaggerated superiority to exaggerated inferiority.

I attempted to show her the falsity of both extremes as expressed in her attitudes toward me as well as in her life in general. I stressed, on the other hand, her fervent wish to find where the truth lay, to search for the essential values of her character. I pointed out to her her compulsion to prove herself superior in accomplishment, at the same time proving herself weak and ineffective. Her insistence upon this constant swing of the pendulum absorbed her whole life. Yet she did not dare to face these facts; and she did not dare to tell the truth about herself. In warning me of her hypocritical tendencies she had hinted that there existed in her a truth which we must discover; that under her lies lay a truth never before admitted. If her lies were for the purpose of creating the impression of superiority or of inferiority, wherein lay the truth?

As a result of this questioning, she exclaimed in the next interview that she had experienced a revelation. She had to her great surprise found herself wondering how a healthy person would feel and act in her circumstances. She had wondered why it was still necessary to prove herself a superior person. If she were healthy, would she not quietly and firmly rearrange her circumstances, finding out what was best for all concerned? She realized that this would necessitate the end of her absorbing confusion and the exercise of clear thinking. She had dreamed of being in a house with her childhood family and her husband. The house caught fire. With great presence of mind she took charge of the situation, organized a fire brigade, and effectively rescued the inmates. The house collapsed but all were saved uninjured. In this dream she was astonished at her lack of anxiety and at the absence of a sense of her own heroism. The possibility of giving up her neurotic attitudes and replacing them with healthy capability now seemed clear and within reach. She determined to examine her present life under this effective lens.

This determination marked the birth of self-control based on self-knowledge gained through experience. Her present search for truth had brought her face to face with alternative modes of functioning, previously unrecognized. In her formative years no such choice had been possible. She had, as a child, unconsciously forced herself into a mold from which there was no escape. She had thereby made herself blind to all alternatives. She had stifled all sense of discrimination and had accepted the inevitable defeat of herself as an individual being. Fortunately this defeat had not been entirely effective. Sufficient leeway remained to enable her now, in her adult years, to re-examine her stultified sense of values, to choose between these values, and on this choice to exercise her reviving will power.

In a later period of analytic treatment the moment comes when the patient has a clear picture of his former neurotic character and also of himself as he wishes to be, as he feels he can be. These two choices in personality and in resulting behavior are constantly in conflict. At moments he is engulfed by his neurosis, at moments he recognizes the neurotic elements and asserts his increasing power to contend with them, and at other moments he experiences the happiness of successfully controlling them. Here we see the battle between the new use of self-control and the yielding to the temptation to lay it aside in order to appease an illusory environment, that of his childhood. Although the more normal alternative brings a glimpse of happiness, it is often accompanied by the anxiety of past experience. This is a time of great emotional stress. The struggle is relieved as he not only consciously decides upon his mode of behavior in thought and action but accepts the responsibility for it.

As an example of this period of treatment we see a young man who has successfully re-entered into active productive life. His many gifts are being exercised; he has made a definite choice of profession; he is enjoying himself. These achievements are the fruit of several years of analytic experience. The last hurdle consists in enabling himself to enjoy others, to take a happy place in social intercourse, to achieve friendship and finally marriage. Having grown up in an atmosphere of hostile domination, his tendency is to believe that all human beings are cruelly possessive. He is comparatively happy when alone, aggressively defensive when with others. His constant state of emotional starvation, of longing to be accepted and loved, propels him into situations of appeasement. In these he loses touch with his own desires and his innate principles. As a result he tends to put himself in the power of everyone with whom he comes in contact. This in turn arouses his self-protective aggression and he loses his new-found friends.

The vicious circle repeats itself continuously, and to live an isolated life seems to him the only solution. His developed insight, however, enables him to recognize the unfortunate outcome of his compulsion and he determines to break the cycle. This can only be accomplished by undergoing experiences which are based on his growing faith that most people are not cruelly dominating but are eager, like himself, to be friendly. Has he the courage and strength to meet such exposure? As he asks himself this question, he tries neurotically to use examples from his experience, in the past and in the present, in order to prove that the lessons of his childhood are correct, that his new insight is false. His everyday life often seems to him to function as a nightmare. People really are moved by hatred and he must beware of them. He is warned and threatened by the misfortunes of his erstwhile friendly relationships. The beneficial outcome of these unhealthy and false situations, which he has himself brought about, lies in his eventual understanding that he invites the sad results. He has been compelling himself to prove that neurotic defense is necessary, that disaster inevitably threatens any exposure of his inherent loving nature.

This new insight strengthens his courage. He recognizes that if he is creating his own unfortunate fate, he can instead create a happy outcome. To do this he must consciously resist his now familiar neurotic impulses; he must give himself the opportunity for happy personal relations; he must control his circumstances. He must choose as friends those who differ from his family, must lay aside his protections, and must assert his loving and cooperative nature. This necessitates a willingness to be responsible for the outcome. He realizes that a mistake is not a fatal failure but an opportunity to learn. He realizes that the fulfillment of his lifelong desire to be loved depends on an exercised and maturing capacity for love.

The determination to fulfill this wish, born of self-knowledge, insight, and experience, functions as a control of himself. He sees the path which he should follow; and he must now force his footsteps along the self-imposed limitations of this path. Only thus can he dominate his fate.

To be a happy and productive person, the neurotic victim must learn to choose effectively between his former blinded functioning and the healthy alternative. His neurotic impulses must be consciously dismissed as destructive. His creative impulses must be eagerly exercised. This is true self-control.

PART IV. Redemption by Love

CHAPTER 11

THE GREAT COMMANDMENTS

"REDEMPTION BY LOVE" is a phrase used in appreciation by a perceptive patient to describe the psychotherapeutic genius of Sándor Ferenczi.[1] It was this gift which assisted in rescuing her from her neurotic way of life, and in finding again the straight path of emotional health which she had forsaken under pressure as a child. This gift remained in her memory for over twenty years as an experience of devotion concentrated upon her return to wholeness. The concern for her as a person, even though the actual therapy with Ferenczi lasted only a few months, worked as leaven and finally culminated in an endeavor on her part, quite alone, to carry out Ferenczi's aims in her behalf. That the victor in this hard-won battle specifies Ferenczi's therapeutic genius as "love" and the process as "redemption" casts light on the similarity of psychotherapeutic love to that love which permeates the Judaeo-Christian faith.

When we study the two commandments "on which hang all the law and the prophets," we see that in both love is the core:

[1] "Recovery from a Long Neurosis," by "Mrs. F. H." (Eleanor M. Burnet), *Psychiatry,* Vol. 15, No. 2, May, 1952. Mrs. Burnet has also given a valuable account of her impressions of Ferenczi in an article entitled "Ferenczi," to be published in the *Psychiatric Quarterly Supplement,* 1954.

in the first, the love of one God; in the second, the love of one's neighbor as one's self. The love of man for God is to be given with complete dedication, complete absorption: "with all thy heart, and with all thy soul, and with all thy mind, and with all thy strength." Implicit in this law is a deep sense of awe and worship for all God's creation, which includes His creature, man.

In the development of the science of psychotherapy, man—man in trouble—is the center of study. His every word and act, his dreams and phantasies, the conscious and unconscious areas of his life, are not only of the essence—all are of equal importance, and are all-important. And, indeed, these segments of the neurotic personality are examined and interpreted by the psychotherapist not as "man-made," but as fulfilling the laws of the government of nature. In truth, one beholds with wonder the marvelous creative power manifested in a neurotic structure. For even the evil aspects of neurosis, of which the patient is ashamed, with which he is guilt-laden, are always found to "make sense." The entire neurosis follows the edicts of natural law. It is in fact and inevitably the consequence of three factors that occur with differing emphasis and in varying patterns in human existence: first, the passionate growth impulse, found in all God's creation; second, the thwarting of this impulse in the presence of other forms of nature, chiefly other human beings; and third, the attempt of the individual to mold his life to these other forms, the attempt to continue in love toward them, in order to persist —although often, alas, neither in full flower nor in the spontaneous and innocent abundance of his full nature. The "sense" that is found in all neurotic organization, even in the elements that may be judged as evil, is that it is always an attempt on the part of the sufferer toward an expression of love—a misconceived love which miscarries.

This human capacity to be and not to be, this capacity to build a whole structure of logical, but false, character and to superimpose it upon the true nature of one's self, as a growing child, is an extraordinary and awe-full power to witness and to examine, to learn to know, to learn to live with, as does the psychotherapist. And he ultimately learns to recognize this structure, from root to branch, as an expression of love. For to love is the essential motivation of growth; to love is the basis of the compromise with overpowering forces, even to the extent of threatened self-destruction; and to love is the cause of the secret preservation of one's inmost being.

Knowledge of the laws of man's nature, whether it is in appearance good or evil, ill or whole, clean-swept or possessed by devils, was startlingly evidenced by Jesus, as he fulfilled the law and the prophets, accurately foretelling the blessed life or the woeful fate of those who listened. Their destiny depended upon their learning to understand and obey these laws. But essential to this task, as to the miracle of healing, is a more basic value. Love of God, faith in God's loving presence—faith, even as a seed of mustard—is the dynamic power which animates man's development. This Jesus demonstrated in all his teachings—by parables, by warnings, by example, and by prayer. He clearly differentiated between the way of life that leads to the growth of the spirit and that which stultifies the spirit. Consecration to the understanding of and obedience to this first way of life leads to the establishment of a loving relationship with God and is therefore the heart of the first and great commandment, that we should *love* the Lord our God with all our heart, with all our soul, with all our mind, and with all our strength.

"And the second is like, namely this, Thou shalt love thy neighbor as thyself." Again love is the core. But the object to be loved in this case is not God but God's creation, man himself. The two commandments are united, closely bound together, as "the Law and the Gospel." How heartening it is that "gospel" means "good news." They are alike in demanding a dedication to the pursuit of a loving relationship—in the second commandment, with man's neighbor. This is to be modeled upon man's loving relationship with himself.

The inference seems clear and inescapable: without love for one's self one is incapable of developing the capacity to love others. Man, through the patient and penetrating study of his own nature, in illness and in health, and of his struggles in living, grows in the capacity to sense in precise detail the needs and conflicts, the desires and disappointments of his neighbor, to put himself accurately in his place. This is the satisfaction of a basic altruistic need in him, a fundamental groundwork for his own emotional and spiritual maturity.

The study must be carried out in love, with man's self as the immediate object. This does not mean any yielding to egoism, self-centeredness, "narcissism." Such self-absorption is a severe distortion of character and results from the deep wounding or loss of self-respect. It represents a perverted attempt at self-healing, by demanding for one's self, by any and all means, all one can get, more than enough, from the environment to compensate for the wound or the loss. This is a thwarting of the growth process, which depends upon giving rather than getting. Rather than self-love, it is an expression of self-hatred. This is in part what Carl Sandburg meant when he pointed sharply to the different kinds of "pride." "I believe in pride, knowing well that the deadliest of the seven deadly sins is named pride. I believe in a pride that prays ever for an awareness of that borderline, where, unless watchful of yourself, you cross over into arrogance, into vanity, into mirror gazing, into misuse and violation of the sacred portions of your personality."

That man's love for himself is distinct from yet closely bound to his love for his neighbor was keenly sensed by D. H. Lawrence, whose article, "Love," evokes comprehensively these most basic human needs:

"There must be brotherly love, a wholeness of humanity. But there must also be pure, separate individuality, separate and proud as a lion or a hawk. There must be both. In the duality lies fulfillment. Man must act in concert with man, creatively and happily. This is greatest happiness. But man must also act separately and distinctly, apart from every other man, single and self-responsible and proud with unquenchable pride, moving for himself without reference to his neighbor. These two movements are opposite, yet they do not negate each other. We have understanding. And if we understand, then we balance perfectly between the two motions, we are single, isolated individuals, we are a great concordant humanity, both, and then the rose of perfection transcends us, the rose of the world which has never yet blossomed, but which will blossom from us when we begin to understand both sides and live in both directions, freely and without fear, following the inmost desires of our body and spirit, which arrive to us out of the unknown. . . . Lastly, there is the love of God; we become whole with God. . . . the Holy Spirit, the unknowable, is single and perfect for us."

And in another article, "We Need One Another," Lawrence continues:

"We have our very individuality in relationship. Let us swallow this important and prickly fact. Apart from our connexions with other people, we are barely individuals, we amount, all of us, to next to nothing. It is in the living touch between us and other people, other lives, other phenomena that we move and have our being. Strip us of our human contacts and of our contact with the living earth and sun, and we are almost bladders of emptiness. Our individuality means nothing. . . .

"And so with men and women. It is in relationship to one another that they have their true individuality and their distinct being; in contact, not out of contact. . . .

"But while we remain healthy and positive, we seek all the time to come into true relationship with other human beings."

In the nature of humanity, as we can see by observing ourselves, there are present three basic emotional elements, three passionate impulses: for self-development, according to individual capacity; for self-expression in creativity, according to individual temperament; and for self-preservation, when threatened with destruction. In order to make use of these beneficent impulses, whether in the pursuit of health or for the remedying of ill-health, whether for one's self or in relation to others, they must be examined and obeyed in the light of man as an individual.

One hint as to this procedure is stressed in both commandments: the single cornerstone of man's life is love. And surely the nature of human love is a chief concern of mankind, a primary subject of investigation. How does love serve as the basic emotional and spiritual current running through human life, as blood courses through the body? How does it influence the fulfilling of the laws of human nature? In what human relationships is love found to function most satisfactorily? How is it then expressed? What causes the failure of this expression? What are the results of such failure? How can this failure be remedied?

Somehow our human mentality shows a greater trust and interest in studying any given circumstance if it is observed in its dys-functioning. We are not inclined to study health as we study illness. Why? It may be through some tendency in man's aesthetic temperament, which does not wish to disturb a perfect and finished performance, but prefers to appreciate, to wonder, to admire. It is usually only the child who pulls apart things that function well. In the case of imperfect functioning, however, the same aesthetic trend insists upon remedying the situation, necessitating an inquiry into and an understanding of the phenomena involved. This course of research is exemplified in the development of psychotherapy.

It may also be that imperfection has an alerting effect upon us, awakening us into remedial activity. Our senses are enlivened, our need to learn is stimulated. The New Testament story brings this possibility acutely to mind. Jesus recognized that the very existence of the spirit could be clearly shown by the power of healing, the power of the spirit over the ills of the body. The disciples were startled by his genius as a healer; the multitude flocked to him. And Jesus succinctly stated, with each miraculous healing, that the cure was the result of spiritual faith. He urged that the miracle be forgotten and that faith be strengthened. In the same way, the probing discussions and parables concerning human relationships and the emotions underlying them had a stimulating, even shocking, effect on his listeners. For the message was strange and difficult to comprehend, being a fulfilling of the true laws of human behavior rather than a routine repetition of well-worn phrases. His followers were forced to think and to question him. His answers led unfailingly to the facts of spiritual development, a new and amazing realm of consciousness.

Illness and sinfulness among human beings seem to act as immediate stimuli for the demand not only for curative measures but for observation and study into the laws beneath them. The answering of this demand leads in turn to the question of the nature of health. In Jesus' terms health of mind, soul, and body is represented by the wholeness of the child, "for of such is the Kingdom of Heaven." If we must become as little children, then surely for those who are ill we must recapture the embracing conditions which have signified health for the infant.

This first experience of loving and being loved—whatever the disastrous misfortunes of childhood—is familiar to each of us; for it has occurred, if only momentarily, in the life history of all human beings. It is native to humanity in the period of gestation and, with good fortune, for a period after birth. We know in the depths of our being, we can sense, this experience of mutuality, even though the memory may be only a trace—and that, unconscious. This fact of human life indicates plainly that the relationship of mother and child, for the light it throws on the maintenance and recovery of health, must be examined, studied, and understood; for it above all others is in essence beneficent and *whole.*

The ideal of therapeutic love is close to the unpossessive, unmanipulative love of the happy self-possessed and self-confident mother for her child: of the mother who is blissful in her maturing life as an individual; blissful in her love relation with the child's father; blissful in her self-completion in motherhood. The sensing of such happiness is a *feeling* experience, an emotional experience, hardly to be defined intellectually. Out of this emotional wealth the mother, both consciously and unconsciously, gives spontaneously to the child whatever he may need at any given moment, for his fulfillment. The gift is an intuitive and instinctive satisfaction of an instinctive need—a need felt by both mother and child. It comes without loss of the mother's integrity as an individual. It is a total response of the mother's self to the self of the child. For the child needs no lesson in loving, as the seed needs no lesson in growth. The plant can be counted upon by the skillful gardener to reach full bloom if given space and air and nourishment. So does the child in its health and happiness answer the mother's devoted care. The flowering of the mother-child relationship is the outcome of mutual and commensurate need, satisfaction, and response.

How can an ideal of the complete maternal gift be likened to that of the psychotherapeutic gift of love? How can we describe the ideal therapist as we have attempted to describe the ideal mother? What is the secret of personality inherent in the gift of healing?

It consists in a quality that issues from an emotional and spiritual capacity to digest and apply in entire beneficence the experiences of life. Its central asset is what E. M. Forster hints at in each of his novels—"a developed heart." The therapist must be a growing personality. He must have discovered for himself a way of life in which he can work toward self-ripening changes and for increasing self-fulfillment. This in itself gives a sense of happy self-possession and self-confidence, from which there flows an ability to identify with others, to sense and to try to satisfy their individual and mutual needs. This is a creative expression of the second commandment: "Thou shalt love thy neighbor *as thyself*."

If the restoration of personal integrity and the self-control gained from this restored integrity are essential goals of psychotherapy, must not the therapist himself in his own maturing process have reached these goals? Must not the training and expert skill which he has acquired be recognized as merely the necessary implements of his profession—important to keep sharpened and in order but in fact only acquisitions added to his temperamental endowment? They are the professional means of expression of his spontaneous and self-disciplined nature, which in turn is devoted to expressing itself in the experience of living. In other words, precept and example, teaching and living, converge and merge indistinguishably in the gifted healing personality.

Thus the psychotherapist subtly speaks through his entire way of life to the patient, teaching him both consciously and unconsciously from the fullness of his own development. Whatever the psychotherapist may accomplish with his patient, he accomplishes because of *who and what he is*. His skill, his empathic capacity, his originality of theory and practice, are the expressions of his integrated, self-controlled, and ripened personality. The difficult task of securing for the patient health and the promise of further maturity, sincerely undertaken and carried through, is in itself, and for both members of the therapeutic endeavor, a delight and happiness.

That the psychotherapeutic relationship is in essence a replica of the mother-child relationship need arouse no surprise nor questioning. God in His plan of creation has given an initial situation which lays the basis for the child's growth. This situation can remain a pertinent and permanent model for assuring the persistence of human health and happiness. It can also indicate the prerequisite remedial measures necessary for the recovery of mental, emotional, and physical health.

If man has strayed from the path of healthy growth into the blind alley of neurosis, thus sinning against himself and others, he must minutely examine each point at which he allowed himself to be turned aside. The anxiety which originally forced him to change his course is reawakened with each step backward. To endure this agony he must needs be accompanied by a simulacrum of the loving parent whom he had always longed to know. Each separation from the path and hence from his true self must be redeemed.

This redemption is activated by man's need to recover his own nature, by his love for himself. It must be accomplished in the recovered ability to love the parental figure of love. In the success of this remedial accomplishment he has obeyed the second great commandment; for he has learned, through the therapeutic study of his self-betrayal, to recapture his wholeness and thus to give to himself the hope and the healing of love. This recovery ensures gratification of his basic need as a child of God: the need to be, even with those who have harmed him, a creator of loving mutuality, a giver of love.

GLOSSARY

NOTE: In this book I have used the terms "psychoanalysis," "analysis," "psychotherapy," and "therapy" interchangeably, as also the terms "psychoanalyst," "analyst," "psychotherapist," and "therapist." The following definitions have been for the most part adapted from those in the *Psychiatric Dictionary* by Leland E. Hinsie, M.D., and Jacob Shatzky, Ph.D., New York, Oxford University Press, 1953.

Anxiety: Exaggerated, unjustified, and intense apprehension precipitated by traumatic situations in the psyche or in the environment; contrasted with "fear."

Association of ideas: See *Free association*.

Auto-suggestion: A therapeutic method, used upon oneself, the purpose of which is the cure of symptoms by the reiterated insistence that they have been rendered nonexistent.

Catatonia: A form of schizophrenia characterized by alternating states of stupor and excitement, or by overactivity together with stereotypy.

Catatonic: See *Catatonia*.

Cathexis: Investment of an object, person, or activity with an emotionally toned interest which gives such object a vital significance.

Compulsion: An action due to an irresistible impulse, contrary to the conscious will of the person; the need to repeat a rationally purposeless act or ritual, though its futility is intellectually realized.

Conversion hysteria: A psychoneurotic disorder in which psychological conflicts are converted and appear in the form of bodily symptoms.

Counter-transference: The attitude produced in response to the transference productions of another person.

Defense mechanism: A means of repression; a character armor which protects the instinctual demands and constitutional temperament from the demands of the frustrating outer world.

Depression: An emotional state ranging from unhappiness to deep despondency, characterized by marked incapacity for pleasurable experience, abnormal lessening of mental activity, and preoccupation with self-abasing ideas.

Ego: An organization of the psyche which functions primarily for the purpose of maintaining contact with and of testing reality.

Empathic: See *Empathy.*

Empathy: The capacity to put oneself, emotionally and intellectually, into the thoughts and feelings of another person; the intuitive ability to sense the living experience of another.

Euphoria: A pathological mental and emotional state of generalized well-being and of elated excitement.

Fixation: The persistent unconscious attachment to certain infantile phases of development.

Free association: A term used to describe a method of bringing into consciousness the contents of the unconscious by means of the spoken reporting of chains of ideas which spontaneously arise when the censor's demand for logical thinking is removed. This process may be free or induced.

Frustration: The prevention of gratification.

Hysteria: A psychoneurotic disorder, characterized by extreme overt anxiety (anxiety hysteria) or by unconscious anxiety converted into physical symptoms (conversion hysteria).

Id: The psychic reservoir of unorganized primitive instinctual impulses, in which the pleasure-unpleasure principle ("pleasure-pain principle") reigns supreme.

Identification: An unconsciously reproduced imitation of the real or imagined character traits of another person; the unconscious incorporation within the psyche of a mental picture of another person.

Infantile sexuality: The normal sexuality of infancy.

Manic-depressive psychosis: A psychosis characterized by periods of extreme excitement and lack of emotional control, with high degree of mental and physical activity (manic phase), alternating with periods of depression. See *Depression.*

Masochism: A term used to denote an emotional state in which the individual is affected pleasurably, often sexually, in suffering pain, ill-treatment, and humiliation, whether inflicted by himself or by others. Often defined as "lust for pain."

Masochistic: Characterized by *Masochism.*

Melancholia: A pathological mental and emotional state, characterized by painful depression, abrogation of interest in the outside world, loss of capacity to love, inhibition of all activity, and lowering of self-regarding feelings.

Narcissism: An excessive and obsessional preoccupation with self to the extent that the capacity for object-love is deficient.

Neurosis: See *Psychoneurosis.*

Neurotic: See *Psychoneurosis.*

Obsession: The excessive focusing on an idea, usually absurd or unimportant, uninfluenced by logic or reason.

Oral frustration: Interference with the infant's achievement of gratification in sucking.

Paranoia: A psychosis presenting delusions of persecution, systematized, and characterized by being clearly defined, coherent, well supported, and defended by the sufferer.

Paranoid: Relating to or resembling paranoia.

Phobia: Neurotic anxiety produced by a specific situation; for example, enclosed places, open spaces, heights.

Phobic: See *Phobia.*

Pleasure-unpleasure principle: The theory that all psychological functioning is determined by the wish for maximal pleasure and minimal pain, for escape from painful situations, and for greatest possible gratification with the smallest effort.

Primal Repression: The task of keeping repressed in the unconscious the material that has never been in consciousness.

Psyche: The totality of mental phenomena, both conscious and unconscious.

Psychoanalysis: The study of the unconscious psychic realm and its relationship to and influence upon the conscious realm; also a form of psychotherapy.

Psychogenic: Originating in the mind or psyche.

Psychoneurosis: Disturbance of personality caused by unconscious mental and emotional conflict.

Psychosis: A severe type of mental and emotional disorder in which the personality is extensively disorganized and contact with reality impaired.

Psychosomatic: Pertaining to a group of disorders or symptoms in which it is assumed that emotional factors play a role in the causation of the bodily disturbances present.

Psychotherapy: The art of treating mental or emotional diseases or disorders by psychological means.

Psychotic: See *Psychosis.*

Rationalization: A reasoning process used to account for or to excuse an unconsciously motivated behavior when the motivation is consciously unacceptable to the person.

Reality situation: The environment appraised objectively.

Regression: The act of returning from a higher level of maturity to an earlier, infantile level of adaptation.

Repetition compulsion: The uncontrollable unconscious impulse to re-enact an early emotional experience of childhood, generally painful and often traumatic, that has remained unresolved. The unconscious aim is to solve the problem.

Repression: The unconscious process of keeping out, banishing from consciousness, ideas or impulses that are unacceptable to the person.

Resistance: The instinctive opposition displayed toward any attempt to lay bare the unconscious.

Sadism: A term used to denote an emotional state in which the individual is affected pleasurably, often sexually, in the infliction of pain and humiliation upon others.

Sadistic: Characterized by *Sadism.*

Schizoid: The term used to denote the aggregate of personality traits known as introversion; namely, quietness, seclusiveness, "shut-in-ness." The schizoid individual separates from his surroundings to a greater or less degree, confining his psychic interests more or less to himself. Not in itself a morbid condition.

Schizophrenia: A group of malignant psychoses, characterized by the blunting of emotions, withdrawal from reality, delusions, and hallucinations.

Sexual impotence: The impairment of male capacity for normal erection, orgasm, or erotic pleasure.

Stereotypy: The constant, usually unconsciously determined, repetition of any action.

Super-ego: The portion of personality which unconsciously echoes the prohibitions and ideals of the significant figures of childhood.

Suppression: The conscious act of concealing or withholding from the sphere of consciousness; contrasted with *Repression,* which takes place unconsciously.

Syndrome: A group of concurrent symptoms which together are indicative of a disease.

Transference: The unconscious reproduction of the forgotten and repressed attitudes toward the significant figures of childhood, and the application of these reproductions to the relationships of later life, more especially to the analyst during analytic therapy.

Trauma: An acute emotional shock that wounds or severely damages the personality.

Traumatic: See *Trauma.*

Traumatogenic: Producing trauma.

Uncathected: See *Cathexis.*

Unconscious, the: A functional system of the psyche, comprising all unconscious mental phenomena, all material not in the immediate field of awareness; consists in perceptions, ideas, emotions, memories, and decisions, of which the person is unaware but which may become conscious.

Voyeurism: Sexual pleasure obtained by looking at the genitals of another; or by "peeping" at any socially forbidden object or activity.

INDEX